CAMPING COOKBOOK

Family fun recipes for cooking over coals and in the flames with Dutch Oven, Foil Packets, and more!

March Raich

WHY YOU SHOULD READ THIS BOOK

Camping is one of the popular activities in the world today. Some fans never hesitate to look for the right ways to get away and enjoy the goodness of nature. When camping, it is important to be well prepared as this will ensure that you can enjoy yourself and enjoy your stay. Many people often wonder what to eat in the wild. This book shows you great ideas that are used by many campers.

TABLE OF CONTENTS

firm, put the lid back on and allow the rest
Dutch oven heat to continue cooking.

A new way to cook bacon and eggs - can work well, though

You use a campfire. The best thing is it doesn't wash of pans afterward.

02

EGGS IN A POCKET

INGREDIENTS

- *brown paper bag / greaseproof paper bag*
- *1 egg*
- *3 slices of bacon*

METHOD

Separate the bacon slices and use them for lining the bottom of the paper bag. After that, break the egg in the bag and fold the top of the bag down twice.

Stick through the bag and hang over the campfire.

The fat in the bacon cooks everything while it heats up.

Don't stay too close to the fire, or your breakfast could be burned.

ADVENTURER'S OVERNIGHT OATS

INGREDIENTS

- *1 cup of oatmeal or steel oatmeal*
- *1 tbsp chia seeds*
- *½ grated apple*
- *½ handful of raisins*
- *1 tbsp pumpkin seeds*
- *1 tsp maple syrup*
- *Sprinkle with cinnamon*
- *Milk of your choice*

METHOD

Oats, chia seeds, grated apple, raisins

Pumpkin seeds, maple syrup, and cinnamon in a glass or airtight container. Mix well.

Pour on the milk of your choice until everything is covered the ingredients. Stir well to make sure everything is soaked.

Three hours in the fridge or overnight, then enjoy it!

COCONUT CHIA OATMEAL

INGREDIENTS

- 1 (425 g) can of coconut milk
- 2 tbsp maple syrup
- 1 cup of oatmeal
- 2 tbsp chia seeds
- ¼ tsp salt
- Mix-ins: berries, banana slices, nuts, Coconut flakes etc.

METHOD

Heat coconut milk and maple syrup in a saucepan until simmering. In a preheated, insulated food container Oats, seeds, salt and all other mix-ins.

Seal and let cook in the pan Container for 30 minutes.

If you want to cook this on a stove instead of a thermos, just add the oats to the boiling coconut milk and cook until

The oatmeal is tender, about 10 minutes.

CHICKPEA BREAKFAST HASH WITH VEGETABLES

INGREDIENTS

- 1 tablespoon of oil
- 1 summer pumpkin or Zucchini cut in ½ inch half moons
- 1 small red onion sliced ¼ inch half moons
- 3 mini peppers cut into ¼ inch slices, or 1 bell pepper
- 1 (425 g) can chickpeas drained
- ½ tsp cumin
- ¼ tsp coriander
- ⅛ tsp cinnamon
- ½ teaspoon salt and more to taste
- 2 eggs

METHOD

Heat the oil in a pan over the campfire or camping stove over medium heat to hot and shimmering.

Add the onions, peppers, and braise zucchini until tender, about 5 minutes.

Add the unload chickpeas and spices and cook until the vegetables and chickpeas are fully cooked and stained brown, about 10 minutes.

Move the vegetables and chickpeas to the sides of the pan to create a well in the middle of the pan.

Add a little oil when the bottom of the pan looks dry.

Put two eggs in the well and prepare your taste.

Take the pan off the oven and serve!

06

BANANA BAOBAB PULP WITH BLUEBERRY-ACAI COMPOTE

INGREDIENTS

Mashed bananas:

- ⅓ cup of gluten-free, organic oats
- 1 cup almond milk
- 1 tbsp almond butter
- 1 teaspoon of Bio Burst Baobab

Blueberry-acai compote:

- ⅓ cup of blueberries
- water spray
- 1 tsp maple syrup
- 1 tsp acai powder

Toppings:

- Dollop coconut yogurt
- 1 tsp chia seeds
- A few nuts
- A few blueberries

METHOD

Prepare the blueberry acai compote;

Add the blueberries, water and maple syrup

Put in a saucepan and warm over low heat until

The blueberries have turned into one delicious jam compote.

Stir in the acai.

Add oats, banana, almond butter, and almond

Put the milk in a saucepan and cook on a low to medium setting heat until the oats are creamy, add some maple syrup

Stir in the baobab.

Top the oats with compote, chia, coconut yogurt, and nuts - very tasty!

07

OATS, BANANAS & CHOC CHIP PANCAKES WITH RASPBERRY COMPOTE

INGREDIENTS

- ½ cup of oatmeal
- 1 cup of buckwheat flour
- ½ tsp baking powder
- 1 large banana - pureed
- Pinch of sea salt
- ⅓ cup of cocoa nibs or milk-free Choc chips
- 1 cup of almond milk
- 1 tbsp maple syrup
- Raspberry compote
- 1 cup of raspberries
- water spray
- 1 tbsp maple syrup

METHOD

Preheat a pan with some coconut oil.

The pan needs are pretty hot.

Add the oatmeal, buckwheat flour, baking powder, cocoa nibs or milk-free choc chips, banana puree, maple syrup (or sweetener of your choice) and put almond milk in a large bowl and stir in thoroughly combine and form a thick dough.

Spoon the mixture one ladle at a time into the pan and fry for 1-2 minutes until the bottom is firm.

Carefully turn the pancakes over and then cook for another one minute or so until the pancakes are cooked through and slightly golden.

Add the raspberries to prepare the raspberry compote.

Put the water and maple syrup in a saucepan and continue to simmer a medium heat until the berries start to melt.

Pour the compote over the stacked pancakes and serve

08

HIGH FIBER MALTY BREAKFAST BAR

INGREDIENTS

- ⅔ cup of gluten-free oats
- ⅓ cup of organic barley flakes
- ¼ cup of quinoa from organic farming
- ¼ cup of sunflower seeds
- ¼ cup of pumpkin seeds
- ½ cup of pecans
- ¼ cup of ground almonds
- ½ cup of flax seeds
- 1 tbspmaca
- ½ tsp cinnamon
- 1 tbsp peanut butter or almond butter
- ¼ cup of melted coconut oil
- ¼ cup of coconut honey
- 2 bananas - pureed

METHOD

Preheat the oven to 5/190 ° C.

Mix all drain ingredients in a large bowl.

Heat coconut oil very carefully in a saucepan until it has melted, then add to the damp mixture.

Add the wet mixture to the mixture and stir well until everything is combined (that shouldn't be too wet).

Line baking sheet with baking paper & spread the mixture on top to an inch thick.

Top with your choice of crispy toppings.

Bake for 25 minutes - test in the middle, cut the bars with a knife to make sure they are cooked. If not, bake for another one a few minutes and test again.

Take out of the oven and let cool slightly and then share in bars.

ABOUT THIS RECIPE

This is the perfect breakfast recipe to prepare you for a day of activities. It requires simple ingredients and is easy to prepare. These fluffy bananas Pancakes are filling, tasty and healthy, and when topped with a honey pot, Berries also makes them a delicious sweet treat.

09

FLUFFY BANANA PANCAKES WITH BERRIES SOAKED IN HONEY

INGREDIENTS

- 2 medium-sized free-range eggs - beaten
- 1 ripe mashed banana
- 130 g of flour
- 1 teaspoon Baking powder
- 130 ml milk
- Coconut oil for frying the pancakes
- Selection of fresh berries - washed
- honey
- Sprinkle with icing sugar to decorate

WHAT YOU WILL NEED

Single gas burner stove

Mixing bowl

wooden spoon

spatula

METHOD

In a mixing bowl, mix the crushed banana, flour, Eggs, baking powder, and milk until a smooth dough is formed.

Melt in a large non-stick pan over medium heat a tablespoon of coconut oil.

Spoon enough pancake batter

Put in the pan to make a medium-sized pancake, let it cook for about two minutes, and then turn over to cook the other side.

Repeat the process until all of the pancake batters are used up consumed, and you have a stack of golden pancakes.

Wash a selection of fresh berries like blueberries,

Put the strawberries and raspberries in a separate bowl.

Large non-stick frying pan

Pour the desired amount of honey over the berries and stir and pour the berries soaked in honey over them on top of the pancake stack. Sprinkle with powdered sugar decorate.

You can also serve them with one or two spoons of Greek yogurt for a refreshing note.

ABOUT THIS RECIPE

It has been proven that oats keep you full for longer. With the addition of coconut, cocoa, dates, and almonds taste more like a decadent dessert than porridge!

DECADENT PORRIDGE

INGREDIENTS

- 75 g of oats
- 6 chopped dates
- 1 tbsp cocoa powder
- 1 tbsp almond flakes
- 2 tablespoons of dried coconut
- 1 tbsp milk powder
- 190 ml of water
- Pinch of salt

What you will need

cooking pot

Storage oven (optional)

Spoon

METHOD

Nuts taste wonderfully roasted, so sprinkle the almonds in one very hot pan and throw until dark brown (this can be done at home), set aside to cool.

All dried ingredients can be mixed together and sealed in one plastic bag. Ideally, the evening before, add the water and let it soak overnight. It can be eaten cold in the morning, though, if you like your hot breakfast.

Use fresh milk, of course, if you have it or your preferred milk alternative. If you like it cute add a pinch of sugar or even better maple syrup or honey

11

POTATO AND PANCAKES

INGREDIENTS

- 400 g mashed potatoes, cold
- 2 eggs
- 1/2 tsp salt
- A pinch of Pepper
- 2 tbsp sunflower oil
- A pinch of Pepper
- 2 tbsp sunflower oil

METHOD

Remove the remaining mashed potatoes from the pan refrigerator and break open something with a fork.

Add the eggs, pepper and salt, to the mashed one Potato and mix.

Heat some oil in a large pan medium heat.

Place a large spoonful of the stew in the pan Bread and spread until the "cake" is that the same thickness everywhere.

Allow to cook for approx. 4 minutes each side to a golden brown and then turn and cook for the same time on the other hand.

Cook until all of the mixture is used up.

Don't overfill the pan and add more oil as you like required.

12

OVERNIGHT APPLE AND CINNAMON OATMEAL

INGREDIENTS

- *50 g organic oats*
- *130 ml almond milk or organic whole milk*
- *A handful of organic sultanas*
- *1 tbsp organic maple syrup*
- *3 roughly chopped organic dates*
- *1/2 an organic apple, grated*
- *A pinch of organic cinnamon*
- *1 / 2½ tsp organic vanilla bean paste*
- *A pinch of salt*
- *Half an organic lemon zest*
- *A pinch of chia seeds*

toppings:

- *Apple compote*
- *flaked almonds*
- *Chia seeds*
- *Roasted pumpkin and sunflower seed*

METHOD

Leave all the ingredients in your fridge overnight (except the toppings) in a jam jar, Kilner jar or plastic container.

When you are about to take your breakfast, take the oats out of the fridge and put it in a bowl with some of the suggested one's coverings.

If the night oats have become too thick, just add a shot before serving. Dies mixture is stored in the refrigerator for up to 48 hours, so you can be a double charge make, about a enjoy some days.

13

QUINOA SUPERFOOD BREAKFAST FRYING PAN

INGREDIENTS

- *2 cups of cooked Quinoa*
- *1 lemon (juice)*
- *Salt price*
- *1 cup of light coconut milk*
- *2 bananas*
- *1 cup of berries (1/2 cup of two types)*
- *1/3 cup of walnuts*
- *1-2 tablespoons of chia seeds*
- *1 tsp vanilla*
- *1-2 tbsp maple syrup*
- *Maca powder (optional)*
- *chopped mint (for garnish)*

METHOD

Remaining Quinoa for this recipe makes it even easier, but if you make it fresh,

Do that first. The recipe is about 2 cups Quinoa, which means you have to start taking it out with 1 cup of dry Quinoa each and 2 cups of water.

When the Quinoa is ready, add it to a large pan along with a price of salt and some lemon juice.

Then add the coconut milk and the banana (sliced)

Set the heat to medium-low and let these ingredients simmer for about 5 minutes, stir occasionally.

NOTE: If you want to prepare fewer calories, alternatively, you can use any other non-milk won't be nearly as creamy.

Next, add all of the remaining ingredients (minus the mint) and give it another 5 minutes to most the coconut milk is absorbed and everything merges wonderfully.

Garnish with some freshly chopped mint leaves and enjoy!

14

CHOCOLATE CHIA PUDDING

INGREDIENTS

- *1/2 cup chia seeds*
- *2 cups of almond and dark chocolate milk or chocolate soy milk*
- *1 tbsp cocoa powder (optional)*
- *1 tbsp maple syrup (optional)*
- *A handful of raspberries (optional)*
- *1 tbsp dried coconut (optional)*

METHOD

Put all ingredients in the bowl and mix immediately.

Pour the mixture into the jars and leave for two hours.

When you're done, sprinkle the Raspberries and coconut on top.

Have fun!

Start your day with a homemade one Breakfast frying pan hash. Packed with nutritious vegetables, Potatoes, Egg, and pancetta, that's all.

15

ASPARAGUS PANCETTA

INGREDIENTS

- *1 tablespoon of oil*
- *Cut 1 medium-sized potato, if peeled, into ¼ Inch cubes*
- *1 bunch of asparagus, cut into 1-inch pieces*
- *115 g pancetta, diced*
- *1 clove of garlic, chopped*
- *¼ tsp sea salt plus more to taste*
- *2 eggs*

WHAT YOU WILL NEED

- *Cast iron pan*
- *Plates*
- *cutlery*

METHOD

You can find rust in your cast iron over a campfire and heating the oil

Put the potatoes in the pan and make sure they are evenly distributed.

Turn occasionally and cook until golden brown (approx. 8 minutes).

Add garlic, sea salt, pancetta, and asparagus and continue cooking for other 8-10 minutes, now when the pancetta is very crispy, and the asparagus is tender.

Make a well in the middle of the pan and crack the eggs, then cook to your preference.

Put on a plate or eat straight from the pan.

ABOUT THIS RECIPE

This recipe feeds four, but if you plan on one exhausting hiking day, or are late on and make this meal so brunch, you may want to double or split the recipe between two. I still can't make it to the end of the year, the second burrito, and it makes me fit for the whole day!

16

BREAKFAST BURRITOS

INGREDIENTS

- 4 tortillas (you can also use pitta bread)
- 6 large closed mushrooms
- 4-8 slices of smoked Bacon
- 2-3 free-range eggs
- 1 medium onion
- Salt pepper
- Ketchup / brown sauce

WHAT YOU WILL NEED

- Single gas burner
- Large pan or wok
- Spray on oil
- chopping board
- Knife
- wooden spoon or spatula

METHOD

First chop your ingredients, also dice the onion (not too small),

Cut the mushrooms into slices and cut the Bacon into bite-size pieces.

Pour some oil into the pan and heat it up.

Gently fry the onions and add the Bacon as soon as it is translucent.

Just add the mushrooms before the Bacon starts to brown.

They become frequent and wait a few minutes for the mushrooms to come boiled, and the water from them has evaporated. Add a little more oil in this stadium if you wish.

Place free-range eggs directly in the pan and mix into the pan Bacon, mushrooms, and onions. Keep them on frying moderately high heat until the Egg is cooked.

Make sure you season it with enough of black Pepper and a pinch of salt.

Divide the contents of the pan into 4 tortillas or flatbreads,

Add ketchup or brown sauce as you like, then enjoy!

17

VITALIZING BREAKFAST GRANOLA

INGREDIENTS

- 560 g of oatmeal
- 150 g of your favorite seeds or nuts
- 1 tsp salt
- ½ tsp cinnamon
- 115 ml of melted coconut or olive oil
- 115 ml maple syrup or honey
- 1 tsp vanilla extract
- 100 g of your favorite dried fruit
- 2 tbsp chia seeds
- 2 tbsp cocoa nibs
- 2 tsp milk powder and water camp

WHAT YOU WILL NEED

- Sheet
- parchment paper
- Large bowl
- wooden spoons
- Airtight container

METHOD

Heat the oven to 200 ° C or 190 ° C when the fan is on. Line a big one baking tray rimmed with baking paper.

Mix oats, nuts, seeds, cinnamon and salt in a large bowl.

Stir to mix.

Pour in oil, maple syrup, or honey-vanilla extract. Mix again to coat everything, pour it into the baking sheet.

 Flatten with the spread the back of the spoon evenly.

Bake for about 20 to 30 minutes, stirring halfway. The time has come

It looks golden brown. Allow cooling completely (this is important because it gets crispy).

Break off with your hands and leave larger pieces if left

They prefer. Shelf life 2 weeks in an airtight container or 3 months in a can Freezer; It's convenient to freeze portions.

When camping, pour some water into a bowl and stir in the powder Milk.

You can heat the milk if you want. Fill in cereal, and enjoy it!

The nuts and seeds from which the muesli is made help make this breakfast really filling - ideal to prepare for the day. Combine with the delicious Mexican hotness Cocoa to make it an enticing pleasure.

18

GRAIN-FREE PUMPKIN SPICE MUESLI WITH MEXICAN HOT COCOA

INGREDIENTS

GRANOLA

- 858 ml in cans pumpkin
- 240 ml tahini (Sesame paste)
- 150 g shredded coconut
- 480 ml coconut cream
- 10 ml vanilla
- 1 tsp each Cinnamon, nutmeg, Ginger, allspice, and clove
- 1 teaspoon freshly grated Ginger or powder ginger
- 120 ml maple syrup
- Raisins
- nuts

COCOA

- 75 g cocoa
- 300 g milk powder

METHOD (MUESLI)

Mix all the ingredients except raisins and nuts in a large bowl.

Spread the mixture on a jelly roll trays in your dehydrator about 1/4 inch (6-7 mm).

The thinner you have it, the more it dries faster, but you want it thick enough that it does a chunky cereal if it is crumbling.

Set the temperature to fruit / Vegetables, and it should take approx. 24 hours (time varies depending on the thickness).

Check some stains periodically on it dries faster than others.

If it dries enough for you can pick up the edges, start to break it into large pieces. However, keep it in the dehydrator until completely dry. Your house will smell incredible!

Once done, crumble in Cereal pieces.

Mount in individual bags with:

- 40 g of sugar

- 1/4 tsp cinnamon

- 1/2 tsp vanilla pod (Optional)

- Pinch of cayenne pepper powder (optional)

WHAT YOU NEED

GRANOLA

- Large bowl

- dehydrator

- Jelly roll trays

- Ziplock bag

COCOA

- Jug

- Ziplock bag

- 75 g of muesli

- 30 g coconut milk powder

- Raisins

- nuts

In stock

To eat cold, just add water cover (approx. 60ml). How to eat?

Pour oatmeal, hot water cover the cereal and let it sit for 5 minutes until softened.

METHOD (COCOA)

Mix the ingredients in a big bowl to break with a spoon Lump if necessary.

If you like it sweeter or want more calories, double the sugar.

You can scratch for the vanilla from inside a vanilla bean

Use pod or vanilla powder.

Store in a jar or ziplock bag. One portion is 40 g mix for everyone 240 ml of water.

You can pack any serving in ziplock bags in snack size for Backpacking.

In stock

Mix in 40g powder mixture

240 ml of hot water each Single serving.

19

SUPERFOOD BERRY BREAKFAST-SMOOTHIE

INGREDIENTS

- 1 banana
- Handful of blueberries
- 160 g frozen mixed fruits
- 140 g of oatmeal
- 2 appointments
- A handful of spinach (promise you don't taste it)
- Almond milk (its depends on amount of how thick you like your smoothie)

WHAT YOU WILL NEED

- Mixer
- Jug

METHOD

Mix all ingredients at once with a blender; you can also use one

Nutri-bullet, but there are many great mixers on the market.

20

OMELETTE QUESADILLAS CAMPSITE

INGREDIENTS:

- One medium of Egg
- One handful of grated cheese of your choice either a Mozzarella or Cheddar any of your favorites.
- One mini tortilla wrap

WHAT YOU WILL NEED:

- Pan
- spatula
- Knife

METHOD

Heat a small pan and crack it, Put the Egg in the pan

Add the cheese immediately while stirring Egg with the cheese with a spatula or similar

Then pan the pan to get the mixture cover the bottom of the pan.

Before the Egg is cooked ready, add a mini tortilla

Wrap up and push down a little to get packing to stick to the omelet

Cook for some minutes until the Egg and the cheese has turned deliciously golden

Turn everything over to crunch the packaging on the table other side or keep it soft if you like

Be able to roll up the packaging for easy eating around the campfire

Cut into pieces and serve with vegetables or immerse yourself in salsa or chili

ABOUT THIS RECIPE

This is a chic pants version of Bacon and eggs that is easy to prepare, regardless of whether you are at a campsite with a large camping stove or outdoors in nature with a Trangia or gas stove.

21

CHORIZO SCRAMBLE

INGREDIENTS:

- One chorizo ring
- 2-3 eggs
- Spring onions
- mushrooms
- Chili (if you dare) or red Pepper (if you feel softer)
- A splash of milk

What you will need:

- Stove
- Pan
- spoons
- Knife & cutting board

METHOD:

Cut your chorizo into coin-sized rings and cut the vegetables into small pieces (the smaller they are, the faster ones they will cook!)

Crack your eggs in a bowl or cup and add a dash of milk and stir very well. You may add a little bit of salt and Pepper if you feel like

Turn on your stove (or have an adult turn it on for you) and put your pan on top

Carefully place the chorizo rings in the pan. You don't need oil for that - if you do Heat up, they release a tasty, natural red oil that you can cook the rest of the dish in the!

As soon as they start releasing the oil, add your oil Vegetables and stir and turn over the chorizo until the vegetables are beautiful and soft

Add the egg mixture and turn the heat deep down. It is important to keep stirring at this stage, so it doesn't Bottom of the pan

Once the eggs are cooked through, it is ready to serve. It is great on its own or with baked beans

22

EASY CHEESY GREEN OMELETTE

INGREDIENTS:

- 3 large free-range eggs
- A pinch of grated cheese (whatever you have, but medium cheddar works well)
- 1 spring onion
- A handful of mushrooms
- A handful of spinach
- Salt & Pepper for seasoning

What you will need:

- bowl
- Scissors
- frying pan
- Fish slice / spatula

METHOD

Place the eggs in a bowl, season with Salt and Pepper, then whisk together with a fork

Add a generous handful of spinach the mixture sprinkle with grated cheese

Chop the spring onions with scissors and drop directly into the mixture

Heat some splash of oil in the pan and let it steep, it heats up a little and then pours into the pan Ingredients. It should hiss immediately and start turning the bottom of the Omelette golden brown

Some people prefer to keep stirring An omelet that you would like to have Scrambled eggs, but you can also leave it to hiss for a few minutes until the bottom is golden brown

Use a piece of fish to turn the omelet over and brown the other side for a few minutes and serve with salad - or just a big blob chic ketchup!

23

FRUITY PANCAKES

INGREDIENTS:

- 4½ ounces of flour
- 2 teaspoons of sugar
- 2 teaspoons of baking soda
- 2 tsp butter
- 4½ ounces of milk
- 1 egg
- 1 tsp oil - for each pancake
- Selection of fruits

WHAT YOU WILL NEED:

- 2 mixing bowls
- frying pan
- spatula
- cutting knife

METHOD

Wash and clean the fruits before cutting. Cut them into thin slices (except Pomegranate that can be sprinkled over the pancake while cooking)

Add milk, Egg and 2 teaspoons. Put melted butter in a bowl and mix together, then jump aside

Put all 'dry' in another bowl Ingredients (the flour, sugar, and baking powder). Mix these together

Bring your "wet" ingredient bowl and add a tablespoon of the 'dry' ingredients mix at a time after each spoon. Mix until all ingredients are smooth Batter without lumps

Add 1 teaspoon of oil in a pan and heat lower the temperature over medium heat

Once the pan is warm, add the dough to the pan and let the spread dough by itself

When the down part of the pancake is cooked (check by carefully lifting with a Spatula), add the fruit slices to the on top of the pancake

Cook for another 2 minutes over low heat.

Turn the pancake to the right for a few seconds before you take it out of the pan

Serve with juice and the rest of the fruit slices

24

OATMEAL

INGREDIENTS:

- Gluten-free oatmeal
- rice flakes
- Dehydrated whole milk. It offers taste, creamy texture and much-needed protein and fat
- A selection of different seeds (sunflower, pumpkin, chia, sesame, etc.)
- Chopped dried fruit - Dates, raisins or cranberries

What you will need:

- Pot
- spoons

- You may also want to add hacked Nuts or other cereal millet flakes

- When you need something extra, try adding cocoa, Cinnamon or your favorite spices

- Fresh bananas provide a fantastic taste sweet. Experiment with your children to create something

Your own version of this camping equipment!

25

RAISIN PANCAKES

INGREDIENTS:

- 80 g raisins
- 100 g self-raising flour
- Pinch of salt
- ½ teaspoon of sugar
- Oil or butter for frying

What you will need:

- frying pan
- Mixing bowl
- spoons
- spatula
- Digital scales

- Mix the ingredients together with enough water so that it will make it thick

- Heat a pan and add a little oil. When the oil is hot, drop spoons of the raisin

Put the dough in the pan and cook on a low heat until solid

- Tip over and cook the other side

- Divide the pancakes between 2 people and sprinkle with some sugar

- If fresh fruit is available, chop it into pieces make a compote and put it on the spoon side of the plate

26

VEGETARIAN ALL-DAY BREAKFAST FRITTATA

INGREDIENTS:

- *6 free-range beaten eggs*
- *4 Quorn Lincolnshire sliced vegetarian sausages*
- *4 slices of Quorn vegetarian bacon, cut in strips*
- *A half sliced handful of cherry tomatoes washed*
- *4-5 cans of new potatoes, drained and cut in half*
- *113 g matured cheddar cheese, grated*
- *Sunflower oil cooking spray*
- *Salt and Pepper for seasoning*
- *Spread sourdough bread slices with olive oil*
- *Spinach and rocket to serve*

What you will need:

- *frying pan*
- *spatula / spoon*

METHOD:

Spray the oil in a large non-stick pan

The entire bottom of the pan is evenly covered

Preheat the pan on a camping stove over medium heat.

Put the Quorn bacon and sausages in the pan and fry until it is fully cooked and golden brown, then set aside

Brush the pan with oil again and fry the cherry tomatoes

Lightly brown the potatoes

Put the Quorn bacon and sausages in the pan and stir

Mix thoroughly with the potatoes and tomatoes

Gradually start pouring the beaten eggs into the pan.

Cover the remaining ingredients thoroughly as well

Sprinkle the cheese evenly over it

While cooking gently tip the pan from side to side

Make sure that the mixture starts to cook continuously

Spatulas to gently push the mixture away from the edges it sets

As soon as the whole frittata appears to be cooked on one side and the mixture is set up so that you can turn it over, take a plate and cover the pan so that you can turn the frittata over and return it to cook the pan on the other side

The cooked side should look golden brown and firm.

Let the other side cook for another 5-7 minutes until the frittata is golden brown and set both sides

Place the frittata on a plate to cool and cut into pieces with sourdough bread slices, cooked, serve Roast olive oil in a pan until golden brown

Serve with a sauce of your choice.

Add some washed leaves of fresh spinach and arugula (if desired)

add a dash of color and fresh taste

27

BANANA & BLUEBERRY PANCAKE STACK

INGREDIENTS:

- 150 g self-raising flour
- 2½ overripe bananas, pureed
- 100 g organic blueberries, washed
- 2 whole eggs
- 1 cup milk (vegetable alternative optional)
- 3 tbsp tasteless cooking oil

Optional extras:

- ¼ tsp cinnamon
- 1 capsule of vanilla extract
- Maple syrup for serving
- Greek or natural yogurt to serve

What you will need:

- Small mixing bowl
- Fork
- Large mixing bowl
- frying pan
- tablespoons
- bowl
- Knife

METHOD:

In a small mixing bowl, crush 2 bananas with a fork. Add the eggs and whisk gently

Sieve the flour and in a larger mixing bowl

Add most blueberries. Pour into the Mix the bananas and whisk again

Now you can use the milk (Cinnamon and Vanilla optional). Mix until everything is smooth and thick

Time for the fun part! Heat the pan with a tablespoon of oil and add a couple of large spoons of pancake mix. Cooking for 1 minute on each side, more oil than add you go with

Put the pancakes in a bowl. Cut the remaining bananas and sprinkle over some blueberries

Enjoy alone or drizzle with Maple Syrup and yogurt

28

AIRY PANCAKES

INGREDIENTS:

- 1 cup of flour
- 1 cup of milk
- 1 medium egg
- 1 teaspoon Baking powder
- A handful of summer berries

What you will need:

- Mixing bowl
- Whisk
- spatula
- trowel
- frying pan

METHOD:

Mix the baking powder and the flour in a bowl together

Add and whisk the egg and half of the milk together

Add the milk while stirring

Create a smooth dough.

You need to add a little more flour to your Batter is too thin. Leave on for a few minutes

Put a thin layer of oil or butter for frying pan and heat over your camping stove

Add a small ladle Dough once the pan is hot it should spread to about 10cm.

Cook them first to make sure the pan is hot enough. The first pancake is not always the best

Cook it for a few minutes until air bubbles form appear on the surface, and the edges are set

Turn the pancake over and cook on top of the other

If you have a large pan, you should be able to make about 3 pancakes at a second time. Continue until you have made it used up all your dough

Serve warm with fresh berries or sliced banana

LUNCH

You can cut and marinate the candy potatoes at home and pack them in one airtight container or bag in your cooler, to save time at your campsite,

29

GRILLED SWEET POTATO FAJITAS

INGREDIENTS

SWEET POTATOES

• 1 large Sweet Potato

• 1 tablespoon of cooking oil

• 2 tsp liquid amino acids or soy sauce

• 1 tablespoon of New Mexico chili powder

• ½ tsp salt

FOR THE VEGETABLES

• 1 red pepper

• 1 poblano or green pepper

• 1 white onion

• 3 tablespoons of cooking oil

• 3 cloves of garlic

• 1 tsp New Mexico chili powder

• 1 tsp ground cumin

• 1 tsp salt

SERVE

METHOD

Prepare and marinate sweet potato steaks:

Cut off the down part of the Sweet Potato. Place the candy

Cut the Potato vertically onto your cutting board and slice it down to create about 4½ "plates.

Prepare the marinade by mixing oil, liquid aminos, Chile Powder, and salt together in a small container.

Place the sweet potato on a large plate and drizzle

Pour the back of half of the marinade over a spoon if necessary to coat evenly. Turn the sweet Potato over and repeat on the other side. Set aside and let it steep for at least 20 minutes.

Prepare vegetables: Meanwhile, slice everything

Vegetables, Peppers, and core. Cut into long strips. Chop the onion into ¼ "wide slices. Chop garlic.

Cooking vegetables: heat over the campfire 2

- *Cut 1 lime into wedges*
- *4-6 flour tortillas or corn for gluten-free*

Tablespoons of oil in a cast-iron pan. Once hot, add the peppers and the onion. Fry on high heat until they soften, then add the garlic and spices.

Keep cooking until the vegetables are tender and the onion is just starting to tan - about 15-20 minutes in total.

Boil the sweet potatoes: right after you get them

Put the vegetables in the pan and place the candy Potatoes on the grill (you can also cook them in a second cast-iron pan if you are not cooking over a pan during your campfire). Cook one side for 5 minutes, then turn and cook the other side for 5 minutes. As soon as you are tender throughout (but not mushy!), pull them

Take off the fire and cut into ¼ "slices. Toast the tortillas over the fire, about 15-20 seconds per side.

Assemble: Place a scoop of vegetables on a tortilla. Add the sweet potatoes and finish with a pinch of lime. Repeat for that other fajitas, and have fun!

30

SIMPLE CLASSIC BEEF BURGER

INGREDIENTS

- 500 g of minced meat on top
- 1 small grated red onion
- 1 clove of garlic
- 1 tbsp ketchup
- Gluten-free Worcester sauce
- Gluten-free Dijon mustard
- Season to taste

METHOD

Mix everything, divide into 10-12 burgers, and cook on each side for 2-5 minutes. Simples!

All you have to do is sit in the comfortable camping chair,

Feet up and sunglasses on, burgers in both hands, look at it for a while ... then have fun!

31

FAST LENTIL & BEAN CHILLI WITH NACHOS

INGREDIENTS

- 1 onion - chopped
- 2 tablespoons of olive oil
- 4 cloves of garlic - sliced
- 1 tsp cumin
- 2 tsp smoked paprika
- ½ tsp cinnamon
- 1 tsp smoked garlic powder (optional)
- ½ teaspoon cayenne pepper
- 2 tsp Harissa paste
- 1 can of organic black drain beans
- 1 can of green organic lentils
- 1 bottle of organic passata
- 1 zucchini - chopped
- 2 organic peppers - chopped
- ½ tsp sea salt
- Black pepper
- 1 tsp maple syrup

METHOD

Put the oil in your saucepan and add the onion.

Fry for 8-10 minutes until tender. Add garlic and season and cook for a few more minutes, then put the vegetables in the pan and fry for 2-3 minutes.

Then add the harissa paste and stir.

Then add the beans, lentils, and passata and simmer for about10 minutes.

Season it with pepper and salt and add the maple syrup and lime. Stir in coriander to serve.

To make the nachos;

Cut the wraps into triangles - then 8 per wrap place on a baking sheet.

Spray with olive oil spray and with smoked peppers.

Bake crispy for 10 minutes.

- *Juice ½ lime*
- *Coriander toppings;*
- *avocado*
- *Handful of olives*
- *Fresh chilies*
- *hummus*
- *Cashew cheese nachos;*
- *2 gluten-free wraps - quinoa and Chia wrap*
- *Olive oil spray*
- *Sprinkle with smoked paprika*

32

AROMATIC TOFU BURGER

INGREDIENTS

- *400 g organic tofu*
- *2 tsp roasted and ground cumin seeds and a pinch of ground cloves*
- *1 tbsp grated ginger*
- *2 tbsp chopped coriander*
- *1 tbsp crispy peanut butter*
- *Season 1 bowl of lime with salt and pepper*
- *1 egg and toasted breadcrumbs to bind*

METHOD

Mix all ingredients and add the Egg

Breadcrumbs bind the mixture to burgers

Cooking on each side takes 2-5 minutes.

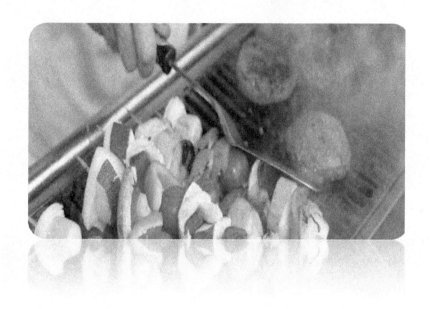

33

FIERY PORK BURGERS

INGREDIENTS

- 500 g of good pork
- 1 inch of grated ginger
- Chinese 5 spice
- 1 hot chili
- 2 tbsp soy sauce
- 1 spring onion and coriander - finely chopped
- Season with salt and pepper

METHOD

Mix together and divide into 10-12 burgers and cook on each side for 2-5 minutes.

As simple as that!

34

CHICKEN BURGER WITH SMOKED PAPRIKA

INGREDIENTS

- Chicken - cut into thin strips and hammer
- ½ lemon juice and lemon peel
- Smoked peppers and spices to taste
- 1 tbsp sesame oil and sesame seeds
- Season with salt and pepper

METHOD

Cover the chicken with all of the ingredients for at least 20 minutes before cooking for 2-5 minutes on each side.

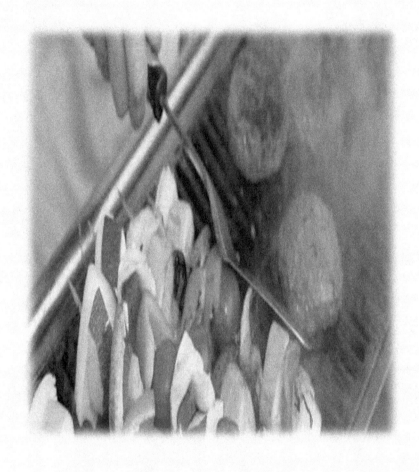

35

RISOTTO WITH SOFT CHEESE & MUSHROOMS

INGREDIENTS

- *140 g rice for risotto*
- *250 g mushrooms*
- *125 g low-fat soft cheese*
- *2 teaspoons of oil*
- *Sea-salt*
- *White pepper*
- *Black sesame seeds*

METHOD

Boil 600 ml of water. Add the rice and stir when it starts to boil, .

Leave on the stove until the rice has boiled. In the meantime, in one Frying pan, heat the oil and throw in the chopped mushrooms.

Cook until the mushrooms are tender.

When the rice is well cooked, take it off the heat and add the spices and the soft cheese. Stir until the cheese is incorporated.

Add the mushrooms and stir it for few times.

36

PASTA WITH VEGETABLES

INGREDIENTS

- 2 small cans of peas
- 1 can of chopped tomatoes
- 320 g dried pasta
- Grated cheddar
- 2 tsp vegetable oil
- basil
- Parsley
- Garlic powder
- Salt
- Pepper
- Black sesame seeds

METHOD

Boil the water and add the pasta.

Make sure you follow the instructions on the pack while cooking.

About 10 minutes when the pasta is cooked, drain the water and rinse with cold water so that the pasta doesn't cook anymore.

Heat the oil in another pan. add the chopped tomatoes, add the spices and let them steep

Let it boil for some minutes and stir from time to time

The bottom of the pan does not get caught. When the tomatoe sauce starts to thicken, add the drained peas and stir.

Put the pasta back in the pan; it boiled in and poured the tomato sauce on top. Stir with care, so the peas don't become mushy. Put the pasta on the plate, add the grated cheddar on top and sprinkle sesame seeds.

37

MOROCCAN CHICKEN PATTIES

INGREDIENTS

- 6 chicken breast cubes
- 2 lemons, halved and juice of 1
- 3 cloves of garlic, crushed
- 1 red chili, halved
- 1 tablespoon of oil
- 150 ml buttermilk
- 2 tsp paprika
- 1 tsp ground cumin
- 1/2 tsp ground ginger
- 1 / 2½ tsp turmeric
- 1/2 tsp ground cinnamon
- A good grind of sea salt and black pepper
- 1 handful of fresh coriander, stems and leaves finely chopped
- Flatbread of your choice

METHOD

Place the chicken in a large seal bag and then add the rest ingredients and massage the bag well combined and the chicken is covered. Let marinate for 2-4 hours.

Build your fire / BBQ and up once

Add temperature to your pan or frying pan to the heat. Then check if it's nice and hot

Add a small amount of the chicken, and when it sizzles, you are ready to go. Add the chicken a spoon at a time so as not to overfill your pan, which will reduce the heat. We want it well and hot, it cooks the chicken thoroughly!

You will see that I have added lemon halves to the marinade, and once cooked, everything becomes charred and the inside jammy. When the dish is ready, press from the meat, and it makes the most delicious addition to the final dish.

Put the pan down from the stove and let it rest for a few minutes

Heat the flatbreads on the fire. Then just serve and enjoy!

38

SUN-DRIED TOMATO AND GIANT COUSCOUS GREEK SALAD

INGREDIENTS

- *A dash of olive oil*
- *300 g sun-dried tomatoes*
- *200 g giant couscous*
- *1 lemon*
- *150 g feta cheese*
- *Salt and pepper*
- *A large handful of fresh basil*

METHOD

Boil a kettle and measure 200 g of giant

Place couscous in a bowl and put a pinch of salt. Fill that bowl to the brim with boiling water, then cover and let it cook for 5 minutes. Meanwhile, chop your sun-dried tomatoes into small bites (or you can break them apart with your hands) and cut them in half your lemon.

As soon as your couscous is cooked – whenever the grain has grown to the size of a BB pellet or a Solero shot - drain and pour into a large tip mixing bowl. Mix with the juice of your lemon and then let a pinch of olive oil cool short time.

After cooling, put your tomatoes in the bowl couscous along with a large handful of basil leaves - that you can tear up with your hands until you add the bowl. Then crumble the feta cheese into the bowl with your fingertips.

Season with salt and pepper.

39

ONE CUP TOMATO AND FETA HEARTY PANCAKES

INGREDIENTS

- 1 cup of self-raising flour
- 1 cup of skimmed milk
- 1 egg
- 4 spring onions, finely chopped
- 1 large handful of cherry tomatoes, quartered
- 100 g feta
- 1 avocado; halved, destroyed and sliced
- Arugula salad
- Salt and pepper

METHOD

Whisk the egg, milk, and flour in a big bowl or container.

Add three quarters of the spring onion, tomato, and feta and stir thoroughly.

Heat a hint of oil in a pan on one medium heat. Spoon with a trowel

Add the mixture to the pan, 1 or 2 spoons at a time (depending on the size of your pan).

If the mixture begins to bubble, use a fish cut into slices to gently turn each pancake and cook on the other side.

Then serve the pancakes on a rocket bed

Sprinkle the remaining tomatoes, feta and spring onions and a pinch of salt and pepper

40

STEW CHICKEN AND CHORIZO RISOTTO

INGREDIENTS

- 1 tablespoon of olive oil
- 1 large chicken breast, diced
- 1 onion, diced
- 2 peppers, sliced
- 2 cloves of garlic, crushed
- 1 tbsp tomato paste
- 75 g chorizo, cut or diced
- 1 teaspoon cayenne pepper
- 1 tsp paprika
- 1 tsp turmeric
- 250 g long grain or risotto rice
- 400 g can of tomatoes
- 400 ml chicken broth
- Splash of lemon juice
- A handful of frozen peas

METHOD

Fry the chicken and onion in olive oil for 5-8 minutes until golden.

Add pepper, garlic, chorizo , and spices and let it cook for 5 minutes before stirring the rice.

Add the tomatoes and chicken broth. Simmer for 20-25 minutes and pop the lid on the pan.

Stir occasionally until the rice is tender.

Make sure it doesn't dry out during the process cook and add more broth if necessary. Once the rice has boiled, a handful of frozen peas before serving.

41

CREAMY VEGETABLE CURRY SOUP

INGREDIENTS

- *1/4 tsp sunflower oil*
- *1 small onion, diced*
- *2 tbsp curry paste (I used Tikka)*
- *300 g peeled potatoes*
- *200 g zucchini*
- *300 g cauliflower*
- *200 ml milk*
- *500 ml vegetable broth*
- *1 tsp sea salt*
- *1/4 tsp black pepper*
- *1 tbsp tomato paste*

METHOD

Dice the onion and add to the soup along with the oil and curry paste.

Stir the onions until they are coated in the curry paste.

Peel your potatoes and cut them very small.

Cut the zucchini into slices and chop the cauliflower in small florets.

Add everyone vegetables to the pan/soup maker along with the rest of the ingredients.

If you are using a soup machine, make it smooth, adjust, and let the machine stand for work.

After the cycle is finished, try to be sure the soup is perfectly smooth; when they are still small

Lump, turn it on to run another cycle.

If you use a pan, cook until the vegetables have softened and then mix with a hand blender or in a liquidator. Assuming you've cut the vegetables fairly small should take these 20 minutes.

42

GRILLED SWEET POTATO POUCHES

INGREDIENTS

- 1 9 inch square of high-performance aluminum foil, lightly buttered
- 2 tablespoons onion, chopped
- 1 peeled and cut sweet potato into pieces ¼ inch
- 1 tbsp melted butter
- 1/2 tsp Worcestershire sauce
- 1 tsp dried parsley flakes
- Season with salt and pepper
- 4 or 5 pecans, roughly broken
- 2 tablespoons of grated cheese (I like a strong one Cheddar)

METHOD

Heat up the outside grill.

Place the potatoe in the middle from butter foil and sprinkle the onion on top.

Whisk the melted butter, Worcestershire sauce, parsley flakes, and season the salt and black pepper. Drizzle that over the top of the potato and onions.

Fold the foil around the potatoes, seal completely.

Then place on the hot grill for 20 to 25 minutes until tender.

Open the top of the foil and sprinkle with the cheese and pecans. BBQ for about

5 minutes longer and let the cheeses melt for lightly roast, then serve hot!

43

FRIED SHRIMP CAULIFLOWER RICE

INGREDIENTS

- *200 g fresh king prawns*
- *1 small cauliflower*
- *2 carrots*
- *300 g can of peas*
- *4 eggs*
- *1 bunch of spring onions*
- *2 cloves of garlic*
- *2 dashes of cooking oil*
- *1 small root of fresh ginger*
- *1 large portion of soy sauce (or Tamari)*
- *1 small portion of sesame oil*
- *Salt and pepper*

METHOD

Start preparing vegetables! Use a grater to shred the cauliflower into coarse pieces of rice grain.

Then cut and dice your carrots; Top and tail your spring onions and chop finely; Peel your garlic and ginger, and chop both finely. Open your peas and drain.

Next, heat a dash of cooking oil in a pan and pat your shrimp dry with a paper towel.

Once your pan is heated up, add your shrimp to the pan along with a pinch of salt and pepper.

Hiss a minute or two before turning over to cook on the other side. After a minute or two, your shrimp are pink all over, remove the pan from the heat, and put the prawns in a bowl.

Cover with foil to keep warm and set aside.

Wipe the pan clean and put it back on the stove with a fresh dash of cooking oil after heating put the carrots, garlic, and ginger in the pan and fry for five minutes to soften your carrot.

Next, add the peas, the grated cauliflower, and ¾ of your spring onion in the pan. Stir everything together and fry for another five minutes.

In the meantime, crack your eggs in a cup and whisk together with a fork.

Add a large amount of soy sauce (or Tamari) and a small amount of sesame oil to the pan; stir into the vegetables until evenly mixed, then spoon everything aside to create a small space in the center of the pan. Turn to low heat and pour your egg mixture in the well in the middle of the pan and then use your fork to climb.

Once your egg mixture is quite firm and messed up, you can mix everything together once; moreover, your eggs spread out in the pan.

Season with salt and pepper and then remove the pan from the heat and spoon your fried cauliflower rice out between bowls to serve

44

CHILLED AVOCADO, WATERCRESS, AND CUCUMBER SOUP

INGREDIENTS

- 1 cucumber; peeled, cored and chopped

- 1 avocado, pulp removed

- 2 small shallots, peeled and chopped

- 1/2 bunch of fresh dill, chopped

- 5 large sprigs of mint, only leaves

- 1/2 sachet of watercress

- juice of 1/2 lemon

- 200 ml plain yogurt

- 150 ml coconut milk (drink, not tinned)

- 1 tbsp extra virgin olive oil

- Salt and pepper to taste

- Sumac and dill fronds for garnish

METHOD

Put all ingredients in the socket blender and flash until you have a smooth one consistency.

Transfer the soup to a container or a bowl chill at least 2 hours before serving.

Garnish with dill fronds and sumac.

45

LENTIL, VEGETABLE AND SAUSAGE SOUP

INGREDIENTS

- *400 g sausages (6 sausages)*
- *1 onion, finely diced*
- *1 celery stick, diced*
- *2 carrots sliced*
- *300 g butternut squash, diced*
- *1 zucchini, diced*
- *150 g green lentils*
- *800 ml broth (I used chicken)*
- *2 tablespoons chopped fresh parsley*
- *1/8 teaspoon black pepper*

METHOD

Cut the sausages into bite-sizes and cook it in a large saucepan until its cooked through and browned on all sides.

Remove the pieces from the pan and place them aside from each other.

There will probably be quite a bit of fat in the pan, so wipe and add all the vegetables and lenses. Cover with the broth and bring it into the broth cook. Bring to the boil and continue to cook

Approximately 20 minutes to the lentils and vegetables are almost done.

Put the sausage back in the pan and cook for another 5 minutes.

46

ROAST CHICKEN WITH PEAS, LEEK AND BACON

INGREDIENTS

- Rapeseed oil for cooking
- 8 boneless, skinless chicken legs, quartered
- Fine sea salt and rough black pepper to taste
- 100 g smoked bacon (3½1 / 2 oz)
- 4 baby leeks, finely chopped
- 240 ml chicken broth (1 cup)
- 60 ml white wine (1/4 cup)
- 300 g frozen baby peas, thawed (2 ¼ Cups, a small pack)
- 1/2 tablespoon of granular Dijon mustard
- 1 baby gem salad, shredded
- A large handful of fresh tarragon, chopped
- A large handful of fresh parsley, chopped

METHOD

Heat the oil in a big pan over a medium-high heat on the BBQ

Season your chicken with salt and black pepper.

Put in the pan and brown all over, removing the pieces as they brown. Add the bacon and cook until crispy.

Reduce the heat and then add the leek cook until they start to soften.

Put the chicken back in the pan and pour over the chicken broth and white wine, then stir together and bring to a simmer.

Cover and let simmer for about 10 minutes with stirring after 5 minutes.

Uncover and add the thawed peas, then stir and recover; to simmer another 5 minutes.

The chicken should be cooked through up to this point, so stir the mustard, lettuce, adjust tarragon and parsley, and spices upon need.

Cover and remove from the heat; let it stand for a few minutes (to wilt the lettuce) and serve!!

ABOUT THIS RECIPE

Enjoy a bubbly, liquid egg yolk every time with this foolproof product

Scottish egg recipe - you will never believe it cooked on the grill!

47

BBQ SCOTCH EGGS

INGREDIENTS

- *1 large egg*
- *3 quality sausages*
- *A piece of blood sausage (optional)*
- *Salt and pepper what you will need*
- *It is best to grill with a lid, gas or charcoal*
- *Pan*
- *chopping board*
- *Cling film*

METHOD

Simmer the egg in water for about 6 minutes and then let it cool in the ice water for an hour before peeling.

Cover the cutting board with cling film and squeeze out the sausage meat on it before tapping to form a large circle.

When using black pudding, crumble the slice on the sausage meat.

Place your egg exactly in the middle of the sausage meat circle and wrap it on and over the egg. Squeeze gently to hold it in place, then roll the Scotch Egg combination in your hands so that the egg is fully covered. Chill for an hour.

Season the Scottish egg with salt and pepper as desired

Then cook on the grill over medium heat with the lid closed for 30-40 minutes or until the sausage meat is fully cooked. Serve your scotch egg warm.

It goes well with mustard and cucumber if you feel like it!

ABOUT THIS RECIPE

If you love Mexican food but want something easier for lunch, then this recipe is perfect for you. The tender cauliflower sets itself apart from the crispy pickled red onions. Top with hot sauce, and you're left with mouth-watering goodness with every bite.

48

CAULIFLOWER TACOS WITH QUICKLY PICKLED RED ONIONS

INGREDIENTS

TACOS

- *1 head of cauliflower, hacked into small bite big florets*
- *½ cup of light lager (or use broth to do this Gluten-free)*
- *2 tbsp cumin*
- *2 teaspoons dried Oregano*
- *1 tsp sea salt*
- *a teaspoon of cayenne pepper*
- *1 tablespoon of olive oil*
- *2 cloves of garlic, chopped*
- *6-8 corn tortillas*

INSERTED ONIONS

METHOD

Let the lime juice, onions, and salt steep in a small bowl for up to 20 minutes. Throw the mixture every five minutes to ensure the onions are evenly coated.

Cook the cauliflower on the pan next to cumin, beer, dried Oregano, cayenne pepper, salt, and garlic until the liquid has evaporated.

Then add the oil and fry the cauliflower until it starts brown.

In the meantime, warm the tortillas on both sides for 20 seconds on each side on the stove burner or your campfire.

Make your tacos by filling each tortilla with the cauliflower and pickled onions, as well as the additional toppings of your choice.

Coriander and hot sauce are great additions if you like hot food!

- *1 small red onion, cut into ¼ inch thick crescents*
- *2 or 3 limes, juiced*
- *¼ tsp sea salt*

TOPPINGS

- *avocado*
- *coriander*
- *Hot sauce*

WHAT YOU WILL NEED

- *Small bowl*
- *pan*
- *stove burner/campfire*

ABOUT THIS RECIPE

This vegetarian dish is full of good things to help your body exercise outdoors. The

Noodles provide carbohydrates from which there is a good protein, the egg in the pasta and the peas and good fat in the Coconut powder. The French onion soup offers great taste and combines everything with a Chinese finish. If you like a little meat in your food, then sliced salami works as does a can of fish such as tuna or mackerel.

49

CHINESE TAKEOUT FOOD

INGREDIENTS

- *90 g egg noodles (or rice)*
- *30 g French onion soup (in powder form)*
- *30 g peas (fresh but dried)*
- *25 g cashew nuts*
- *2 tsp coconut powder / flour*
- *Splashes of Tabasco*
- *Sprinkle of soy sauce*

WHAT YOU WILL NEED

- *Cooking pot*
- *Camping stove*
- *Spork*

METHOD

The cashew nuts taste good if you first roast them in a bowl at home in a hot, dry pan (no oil required).

Cook it according to the manufacturer's instructions.

When you're done, the noodles should only sit in enough water add a little more for the French onion soup if it is too dry.

Pour the soup, coconut powder and simmer accordingly Instructions; this should thicken nicely to make a sauce.

Add the peas and cashew nuts for just a minute.

Add the soy sauce and tabasco to taste.

50

FORAGED SHELLS

INGREDIENTS

- 4 chopped strips of bacon
- 1 small onion, finely chopped
- 2 medium cloves of garlic, chopped
- 330 ml of good local ale
- bought about 80 feeds or 2 pounds, fresh mussels scrubbed clean, and beards / Barnacles removed
- Salt and freshly ground black pepper
- A handful of chopped parsley leaves
- Crispbread to serve

WHAT YOU WILL NEED

- Bucket/bag for collecting shells
- Large pan with lid
- spatula
- Knife
- chopping board
- paper towels
- Large bowl

METHOD

Place the bacon in a large pan and cook over medium heat, occasionally stirring to brown and crispy. It will take around 5 to 7 minutes. Then line a plate with paper towels and transfer the bacon with a slotted spoon. Lay on one side.

Stir the onion and garlic in the pan for about 3 to 5 minutes or until they soften and start to tan. Pour in the beer and stir until it begins to bubble, reduce the heat, and add the cleaned one Shellfish. Simmer for 5 minutes with the lid closed.

Check the shells. If any of them are open, transfer them to a large bowl. Simmer for a further 5 minutes and repeat the last step.

Discard closed or damaged mussels and season with the sauce salt and black pepper. Pour over the mussels and top with bacon and chopped parsley.

Use crispy bread to wipe the sauce and serve with a cold, refreshing beer.

SURF HACK: No beer on hand? You can use the same amount of seawater and a dash of lemon juice for a spicy finish. Don't like beer? Experiment with wine, or coconut milk and chili.

51

ROSEMARY AND ONION FOCACCIA

INGREDIENTS

- 245 g of white bread flour, in addition to dusting
- 70 g of finely ground semolina flour
- 1 packet of dry yeast
- ½ tbsp honey
- 280 ml of lukewarm water
- Sea-salt
- olive oil
- Extra virgin olive oil
- 1 red onion, finely chopped
- 3 or 4 sprigs of fresh rosemary

WHAT YOU WILL NEED

- Cast iron pan
- pan
- Foil
- Large bowl
- Fork
- Cling film

METHOD

Put ½ teaspoon of sea salt and put the flour in a large bowl and make a fountain in the middle.

Mix yeast, honey, and lukewarm water and leave for a few minutes until the yeast starts then pour in slowly to foam the flour well.

Mix with a fork as you do that wait about a minute for the ingredients to come together and form a ball.

Flour lightly a surface and knead the ball for about 5 minutes to smooth. If you find the dough is still very sticky, add a little more flour.

Use olive oil to line a large bowl and put the dough in the bowl, then make sure you cover it with oiled cling film and a damp towel and space for a warm place for an hour.

As soon as the dough has doubled, you can choose your size BBQ over medium heat.

 Place skillet over the heat and pour in 2 tablespoons of olive oil then fry the onions very well until they become soft and light brown.

Take off the stove and let it cool and lightly oil the cast iron frying pan.

Set up your BBQ or grill for offset or indirect heat around 375F.

Put the dough in a pan and press until it fills it.

Use your fingers to create a small crater in the batter.

Sprinkle onions and rosemary leaves on the dough and pour in a small amount of olive oil on top.

Sprinkle with a little sea salt over the finished bread and cover the pan with foil.

Bake on the grill on the unlit side for 20 minutes or until brown. Turn the pan evenly browning.

As soon as it is cold, slice, serve and enjoy!

DINNER

A quick and easy meal to eat with lunch or dinner in just a few minutes!

52

LEMON AND TARRAGON CHICKEN SALAD

INGREDIENTS

- *1 pack of cabbage schnitzel (Coleslaw)*
- *1 can or a pack of cooked Chicken (omit for vegans)*
- *½ cup of sunflower seeds*
- *1 lemon - juiced*
- *3 tablespoons of olive oil*
- *1 tsp fresh or dry tarragon*
- *Sea-salt*

WHAT YOU WILL NEED

4L sealable food bag

knife

METHOD

Put the cabbage, Chicken, and sunflower seeds in a bowl 4L closable grocery bag and throw.

Squeeze the lemon juice into the bag and add the oil and tarragon. Throw again to distribute the dressing.

Salt to taste to make 6 servings.

ABOUT THIS RECIPE

This is a great meal to prepare outside as you only need one pot: a Can opener and a camping stove! The heat from the chili will warm you up from the inside if you're eating it at night time or if you're thinking of doing it for lunch, the chocolate will be a cheeky bit of energy to help you continue on your adventure!

53

PALEO CHILI CON CARNE

INGREDIENTS

- 1 can of chopped tomatoes
- 500 g minced beef or pork
- 2 large handfuls of mushrooms - chopped
- Bacon if you have it - chopped
- Green vegetables such as broccoli, kale, green peppers
- 1 red pepper - chopped
- 2 tsp paprika
- 1 onion, diced
- 4 cloves of garlic, finely chopped
- Olive or coconut oil for frying
- 25 g dark chocolate
- Pair of fresh tomatoes to serve (optional)

METHOD

Heat your coconut or olive oil in a large pan.

Add onions and garlic 3 minutes on low.

Add the minced meat and bacon if you have it and still brown it for about 5 minutes on low.

Add the tomatoes, peppers, and chili and bring to a boil.

Turn it down and add vegetables and chocolate.

Simmer for 12 minutes.

Season to taste.

• *Avocado for serving (optional)*

• *Natural yogurt/coconut yogurt for storage to serve it paleo (optional)*

The delicious triangular leek has mild aromas of spring onions and sweet garlic. It is a very invasive, non-native pest landscape a favor and chows down!

54

WILD LEEK BHAJI BURGER

INGREDIENTS

- *70 g triangular leek (or spring onion)*
- *1 tsp ground coriander*
- *1 tsp garam masala*
- *70 g of flour*
- *½ tsp salt*
- *100 ml sunflower oil*

WHAT YOU WILL NEED

2 bowls

Swing

Tongs / spoons

METHOD

Wash your leek, but don't worry about drying. Tearing in about 5 cm long, put in a bowl and massage in the salt,

Let it rest for 20 minutes. The salt removes moisture. This helps the gram of flour to form a dough.

In another bowl, mix your flour and spices, and when the leeks have had 20 minutes, gradually add the flour mix and massage into the leeks until all has been added.

Keep that in mind leeks will not float in the dough, just covered with sticky grams flour. Divide the stew into two parts and shape them into thin patties.

Warm your oil over medium heat and add a piece of leek to test it sizzles.

Fry your bhajis flat for 3-4 minutes at a time side or until golden and crispy. Serve in toasted bun raita and mango chutney.

55

WILD PAELLA

INGREDIENTS

- *1 tablespoon of olive oil*
- *1 medium onion*
- *2 red or yellow peppers*
- *100 g green beans*
- *300 g paella rice*
- *1 tsp smoked paprika*
- *1 tbsp tomato paste*
- *A small glass of white wine*
- *1 liter of chicken broth*
- *1 lemon*
- *A handful of fresh parsley*
- *A handful of wild garlic*
- *shrimp*

WHAT YOU WILL NEED

Big pan

spoon

Push net

METHOD

Rinse the shrimp in fresh water, and bring to boil water, boil for about 3-5 minutes.

Heat the oil in a pan with medium heat, chop and add Onions and peppers. Let cook for 15 minutes until the Onions have softened without coloring.

Slide the onion and pepper mixture onto one side of the pan and add the tomato puree and fry for a few minutes to increase the depth Taste.

Add the smoked paprika and stir.

Add white wine and stir, simmer for 1 minute.

Add the rice and most of the chicken broth (preserving 100 ml for later) and stir.

Let it cook for 15 minutes or until the rice is tender. Add a little stock if it is drying out too soon.

Stir in fresh tomatoes, Beans, and shrimp. Put the cover back and cook for another 6 minutes or until almost the entire stock has been taken up — text to season and add if necessary.

Squeeze the lemon juice all over and scatter chopped wild garlic and parsley to serve.

56

HEALTHY SWEET CHILLI PRAWN/ QUORN STIR FRY

INGREDIENTS

- Fresh sprouts
- Pre-cooked fresh pasta
- Fresh, sweet chili sauce
- King prawns or Quorn pieces
- Pre-chopped bag of mixed pan vegetables
- Olive oil spray

METHOD

Use a large skillet or wok and add a few sprays of oil to it.

Graft in vegetables and cook over medium to high heat a few minutes until they soften and get some color.

If you are using Quorn parts, add them now cooked pasta and stir for a few more minutes to heat them.

Finally, add the chili gravy. If you use shrimp, watch them for a few minutes.

57

CAMP CASSEROLE - STEAK / QUORN

INGREDIENTS

- Leek
- mushrooms
- carrots
- celery
- Beef or vegetable broth
- red wine (optional)
- Lean steak cut into pieces or 1 bag of Quorn pieces
- Corn flour or low-fat crème fraîche
- New potatoes
- Herbs & Spices - Rosemary, Thyme, bay leaf, and pepper

METHOD

Cut the vegetables into pieces. Hack the small new potatoes in half. Do the share and heat slightly, adding some red wine. Add herbs and season. Add the chopped vegetables and potatoes. Pop in your chopped steak or Quorn pieces. Slow cook for at least 3 hours.

If you cook this meal while

Camping when you can't simmer an open fire or on a wood stove, you can cook all of your ingredients individually before adding to the inventory and simmer for 15 minutes. That will save time, and you don't need to let the pot simmer for hours

Compromise on the depth of taste; however, be sure to add an additional one's season as needed.

58

SPICY BEAN BAKE

INGREDIENTS

- 1 tsp vegetable oil
- 400 g bacon
- 2 cloves of garlic
- 2 medium-sized onions
- 1 can of 5 bean salad
- 1 can of chopped tomatoes
- 360 g rice
- Tortilla chips
- sour cream (optional)

WHAT YOU WILL NEED

Dulcimer knife

Frying pan pot

Double burner camping stove

METHOD

This dish can be done all in one swing over a camping stove.

Chop the bacon, onion, and garlic, add them to the can and fry until the bacon is cooked over, and the onions are soft. In the meantime, cook the rice in a pan.

Cook according to the directive on the package 90-100 g rice per person.

If the onions, bacon, and garlic be cooked, pour in five cans of bean salad and chopped tomatoes.

Bring to the boil, then decrease the warmth and let simmer until the beans are cooked through. Serve with rice and tortilla.

59

BBQ THREE PIECES OF CHEESE PORTOBELLO MUSHROOMS

INGREDIENTS

- 20 g grated Italian hard cheese
- 50 g brioche - crushed
- 100 g cream cheese
- 100 g grated cheddar cheese
- 1 lemon juice
- 10 g finely chopped fresh coriander
- 2 finely chopped spring onions
- Salt and pepper
- As many Portobello mushrooms as you like!

METHOD

Peel the mushrooms, rinse lightly and remove the stems.

Absorb water.

Mix all the ingredients listed below in a bowl and mix well.

Don't hesitate to try and optimize the recipe if you like.

More zing just add additional lemon juice.

Add about a large teaspoon of the mixture to each mushroom and cook on a plancha on your grill or in your wood stove for approx 10-15 minutes, depending on the kit.

BBQ Whiskey Oak smoked beef carpaccio

60

BBQ WHISKEY OAK SMOKED BEEF CARPACCIO

INGREDIENTS

- 1 fillet of high-quality beef - remove all excess fat
- 1 mashed garlic clove
- 1 tbsp fresh coriander - finely chopped
- 1 tbsp fresh thyme - finely chopped
- 3 tablespoons of olive oil
- 1 tbsp sea salt
- 1 tablespoon of freshly ground pepper
- Soaked whiskey oak chips

METHOD

Brush your fillet with pepper and salt and Get your grill up to 75/100 ° C, add your pre-soaked whiskey oak chips, and let smoking your fillet on indirect heat, e.g. 30 minutes.

Mix all the elements in a bowl and then rub the whole fillet and let it steep.

Let it rest for 20 minutes.

Now it's time to punch your carpaccio:

Get your grill up to 600 ° C plus and sear each side of your beef fillet 3-4 minutes on a cast iron pan.

Take the fillet off the stove and let it go cool to room temperature.

Cut as thin or thick as you want

Drizzle with lemon juice and sprinkle parmesan cheese.

If you want to cut your carpaccio into thin slices, wrap in cling film and freeze overnight, that is, it is much easier to cut.

61

VEGAN BULGUR CHILI

INGREDIENTS

- *1 tablespoon of olive oil*
- *1 red onion - diced*
- *1 red pepper - chopped*
- *1 can (400 g) diced tomatoes*
- *¾ cup of quick-cooking bulgur*
- *1 tsp Mexican spice*
- *Salt to taste*
- *Sugar at will*
- *1 can (400 g) kidney beans - drained*
- *4 pieces of dark chocolate (70% cocoa)*

WHAT YOU WILL NEED

Cutting board, knife, pot, Spatula or spoon

METHOD

Warmth the olive oil in a pot on medium heat. Cook carefully

Stir the onion gently, stirring constantly. Stir in the red bell

Paprika, bulgur, and Mexican spices. Heat together for a few minutes.

Pour into diced tomatoes and 1 cup of water; bring to a boil: season too and taste.

Add the kidney beans and warm for 6–7 minutes until the bulgur is tender and almost all of the liquid is absorbed.

Stir in chocolate pieces and enjoy!

62

RED LENTILS & COCONUT DAL WITH ROASTED SUNFLOWER SEEDS

INGREDIENTS

- 1 tbsp coconut oil
- 2 small onions - chopped
- 1 tsp mustard seeds
- 1 tsp cumin
- 1 tsp turmeric
- 1 tsp ground coriander
- ½ tsp chili flakes
- 1 cup of red lentils
- 5 cups of water
- 1 cup of dried coconut
- 1 tsp sea salt
- 1 cup of sunflower seeds

METHOD

Place the onion with the coconut oil in a large pan and fry on low heat for 10 minutes.

Add to that spices and fry for a few more minutes.

Wash the lenses thoroughly and drain them.

Next, add the water and the lentils to the pan and simmer for 15 minutes over low heat.

Finally, stir in the coconut and season with salt and pepper.

Roast the sunflower seeds in a dry pan (medium size).

Heat for a few minutes.

Throw them occasionally and keep an eye on them because they burn quickly!

Serve the top with roasted sunflower seeds.

63

SMOKY BEAN CHILLI

INGREDIENTS

- *1 can of kidney beans*
- *1 can of chopped tomatoes*
- *1 can of butter beans*
- *1 can of black beans*
- *1 can of black beans*
- *1 heaping tablespoon of tahini*
- *1 tbsp chipotle paste*
- *1 tablespoon of chili powder*
- *1 large red onion*
- *2 red peppers*
- *2 cloves of garlic*
- *Large pinch of tomato paste*
- *Salt and pepper for seasoning*

METHOD

First, chop the onion and garlic and add them to a deep frying pan or saucepan.

Fry in a little oil.

While they boil, rinse and drain the beans.

Add your chopped red pepper, so touching that nothing burns

Then add the beans to the mixture.

Add your chipotle paste and chili powder and coat the beans.

After coating, pour the tomato and puree and turn the heat down low.

Then stir in your tahini and mix it thoroughly.

Let the chili warm for about 25 minutes

Let the edges of the pan started to become crispy (best pieces!) and serve.

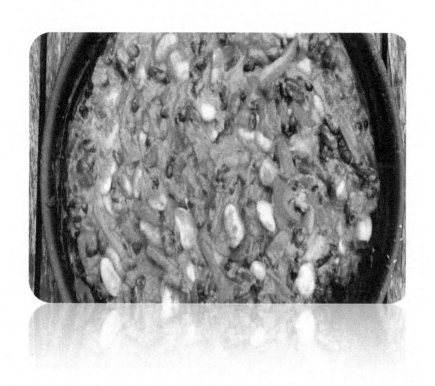

64

CHICKEN AND SPINACH CURRY

INGREDIENTS

- 1/4 tsp cumin
- 1 tsp ginger
- 1 tsp coriander
- 1 tsp fennel
- 1/4 tsp cumin
- 1 tsp chili
- 1/2 tsp garam masala
- 500 g spinach
- 3 tablespoons of oil
- 500 g chicken cubes
- 3 tbsp tomato paste
- 1 tsp arrowroot (optional)
- Salt

METHOD

Wash the spinach and drain until the water is out Path.

Heat 1 tablespoon of oil in a saucepan at medium heat.

Add spinach leaves

1/2 teaspoon of salt and cook for 3-4 minutes.

Heat the remaining oil in your saucepan

Add whole spices over medium heat sizzle.

Then add the chicken and salt in front of you and cover and let cook for 5-8 minutes.

Add your ground spices and stir.

Add tomato paste and sauté a few minutes ago

Add 300 ml of water with 1 teaspoon of arrowroot.

Cover and cook for 30 minutes, then add spinach and cook for 40-50 minutes in the low boiling heat.

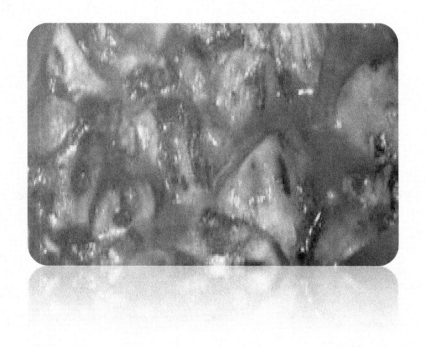

65

STEW WITH SWEET POTATOES AND PEANUTS

INGREDIENT

- 3-5 sweet potatoes
- 2 onions
- 2 tbsp peanut butter
- 3 cloves of garlic
- 1 thumb-sized piece of ginger
- 1 red chili
- 1 tsp cumin
- 1 teaspoon cayenne pepper chili powder
- 2 cans of coconut milk
- 2 handfuls of unsalted peanuts
- 6 blocks of frozen spinach
- 1 lime
- 1 bunch of coriander
- Sea-salt
- Black pepper
- Olive oil
- 2 large flatbreads

METHOD

Peel and chop onions, garlic and onion ginger, then wash and chop your sweet

Cut the potatoes into bite-size pieces.

Heat a pinch of olive oil in a pan and cook your onions gently at a medium to low level

Heat for 6-8 minutes until soft.

Add garlic, ginger, cumin, sweet potatoes and chili

Powder, and cook for another 2 minutes.

Stir in and pour in peanut butter

Your coconut milk. Half fill the coconut milk

Deglaze with water and add to the pan

Stir and simmer for 30 minutes until potatoes are soft.

Add your spinach for the last 10 minutes.

While it is boiling, you can do it

Your topping-out ceremony! Inspire the lime to start with

Then fry the peanuts in a pan (at a low setting)

Heat for 1-2 minutes until light brown but not burned.

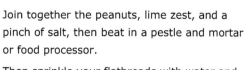

Join together the peanuts, lime zest, and a pinch of salt, then beat in a pestle and mortar or food processor.

Then sprinkle your flatbreads with water and heat up in the oven.

Finely chop the coriander and add the stew.

Press in the lime juice

Season with salt and serve in a bowl with your toppings and flatbread page. Enjoy!

66

LEMON AND GARLIC PRAWNS

INGREDIENTS

- 1 tablespoon of olive oil
- 1 piece of butter
- 2 cloves of garlic, crushed
- 8 raw langoustines
- Juice from 1 lemon
- 2 tablespoons of dry wormwood
- Handful of fresh parsley, fine chopped
- Extra lemon if you want

• METHOD

As soon as the fire has started to sink, but still is pretty hot, put your pan on the grill. When hot

Add the oil, butter, and garlic and then add the langoustines immediately.

Let each side cook for 5 minutes, then add wormwood and lemon juice and let bubble gone for another minute or so.

67

STEW OF SWEET PAPRIKA CHICKEN

INGREDIENTS

- 4 free-range chicken breast fillets
- Chorizo
- 2 medium-sized onions
- 1/2 glass of roasted peppers or 1-2 whole fresh peppers depending on your preference
- Smoked peppers
- 3 cloves of garlic (chopped)
- A pinch of cayenne pepper
- 500 g of passata
- 1 can of chopped tomatoes
- Olive oil
- 1 + 1/2 cups of paella rice

METHOD

Cut the onions and roasted peppers into slices and add

them in the pan with a pinch of olive oil sweat off.

Slice the chicken breast and chorizo.

Add swivel and lightly fry at a very low setting heat.

Put the chopped garlic in the bowl.

Add the passata and chopped tomatoes

Add a few pinches of chili flakes or cayenne pepper.

Add at least 1 heaped teaspoon of smoked product Paprika.

Put paella rice in the pan and fill with a little water as needed to prevent the dishes from drying out.

Simmer on little heat for 45 minutes or cook slowly for a few hours around the campfire.

This one-pot recipe is full of ingredients rich in antioxidants, making it a particularly nutritious dinner spent outdoors after the day.

68

SUPERFOOD STEW

INGREDIENTS

- *1 tsp olive oil*
- *1 tsp cumin*
- *1 tsp turmeric*
- *2 leeks*
- *2 cloves of garlic*
- *2 cm fresh ginger*
- *Pinch of salt*
- *400 g kidney beans*
- *500 g of passata*
- *2 or 3 sprigs of rosemary*
- *2 carrots*
- *2 sweet potatoes*
- *A handful of broccoli*
- *A handful of cauliflower*
- *A handful of kale*
- *50 g quinoa*
- *800 ml vegetable broth*

METHOD

Brown the leek in a little olive oil for a few minutes until they are soft.

Add the garlic, ginger and dry spices and fry for a few minutes longer.

Add any remaining ingredients of kale.

Bring to a boil, then reduce

Simmer for 30 minutes or until when the vegetables are cooked gently.

Add the kale 5 minutes before serving.

This vegetarian chili is very filling and tasty, and the barbecue sauce adds a sweet and smoky depth to taste.

This is a quick and easy campfire dinner.

69

SPICY BEAN PEPPERS WITH PAN-FRIED TORTILLAS

INGREDIENTS

- 4 tablespoons of olive Oil
- 4 tortilla wraps (one per person)
- 1 medium-sized onion, diced
- 4 tsp mild chili powder (use this as a guide, however, decrease or increase depending on how spicy you like Yourchilli!)
- 1 can of cannellini beans, drained
- 1 can of red kidney beans, drained
- 2 cans of chopped tomatoes
- 300 g vegetarian minced meat
- 2 boxes with 500 g tomato passata each

METHOD

Cut the tortilla wraps into triangles to shape them

Warmth 2 tablespoons of olive Oil in it

Fry the pan and tortillas until golden brown

Brown on both sides, half crazy.

Once the tortillas are ready, set them aside cool.

Dice the onion and heat the remaining olive Oil in the pan over medium heat.

Fry the onion until softened, then add the mild chili powder and stir well to brush the onions.

Add the 2 cans of beans, the tomato passata and put the 2 cans of chopped tomatoes in the pan and stir well.

 Add the vegetarian minced meat and the grill

Add the sauce to the chili and stir again.

Simmer on medium heat for 20 minutes until the chili is thoroughly heated and thickened.

- *4 tbsp high quality grill sauce*
- *Grated cheese and crème Fraiche Serve*

Serve with grated cheese and crème Fraiche with a side of the homemade tortillas!

70

SHAKSHUKA

INGREDIENTS

- *1 glass of roasted peppers in Oil (approx. 280 g)*
- *1 large onion, thinly sliced*
- *2 cloves of garlic, chopped*
- *1 tsp coriander*
- *1 tsp paprika*
- *1/2 tsp cumin*
- *1/2 tsp cayenne pepper*
- *1 tbsp harissa*
- *400 g canned tomatoes*
- *4 free-range eggs*
- *2 tablespoons fresh parsley, roughly chopped*
- *Salt and pepper*

METHOD

Drain the paprika and keep 1 tablespoon of Oil.

Warmth the Oil in a heavy-bottomed pan (ideally poured iron) and fry the onion for 10 minutes until it is soft and starts to tan.

Add the chopped garlic and fry it fragrant.

Put the spices and harissa in the pan and a few minutes with constant stirring so that they do not burn.

Cut the roasted peppers into large slices and add pan, along with the canned tomatoes.

If your tinned tomatoes are perfect, break them up a bit with a wood Spoon. Stir everything well.

Warm the sauce over low heat for about 10 minutes

Leave on for minutes, but do not dry. Even if it looks like it dry, add a splash of water.

Use the back of a spoon to add 4 wells to the sauce then just crack the eggs one by one.

Let simmer until the eggs are white solidifies, but the egg yolk is still running.

Season with salt and pepper, distribute the minced meat

Pour parsley over it and serve directly from the fresh pan bread and greek yogurt if you have it.

71

SWEET POTATO, CAULIFLOWER, AND PEANUT STEW

INGREDIENTS

- 6 shallots, roughly chopped
- 1 tablespoon of olive oil
- 4 cloves of garlic, sliced
- 1 tsp cumin
- 1 tsp turmeric
- 6 tomatoes, chopped
- 1 can of organic coconut milk
- 1 cup of water
- 1 sweet potato, peeled and diced
- 1 small cauliflower, chopped
- 1 tsp sea salt
- 3 tbsp crispy peanut butter
- 1/2 lime juice
- 1 tsp tamari
- Chilli flakes
- Roasted peanuts
- coriander

METHOD

Put the oil in a large pan with a lid and heat to medium heat, then add to the pan Shallots. Approximately 8-10 minutes to soft and browning.

Add garlic, cumin, and turmeric and Coriander. Stir for 30 seconds.

Next, add the hash tomatoes and cook for another 5-6 minutes; then add the water, coconut milk, sweet potatoes, and cauliflower.

Warm for 20 minutes with the lid closed until the sweet potatoes and cauliflower are tender.

Whisk in the lime juice tamari, chili flakes, salt, peanut butter, and pepper. Simmer for a few minutes.

Top with roasted peanuts and fresh Coriander.

72

ROSEMARY ROASTED VEGGIES WITH TURKEY AND PECANS

INGREDIENTS

- *4 cups of diced root vegetables (Carrots, parsnips, and sweet Potato)*
- *1 cup of roughly chopped onion*
- *3 cloves of garlic, crushed*
- *1/4 cup of oil (avocado or Coconut)*
- *1-2 cups of water*
- *1 cup of cooked turkey*
- *1 cup of pecans*
- *1/2 cup of dried cranberries*
- *1 tsp salt*
- *1 tsp dried rosemary*

METHOD

(AT HOME)

Chop the vegetables and onions put in a container with the garlic. Mix the pecans, cranberries, and spices together and put them in a separate container.

For Turkey, you can use leftovers or cut them up prefabricated, cooked turkey pate.

Keep in one airtight container in the cooler, or it will take time a day or two without cooling.

(IN CAMPING)

Prepare the campfire with the briquettes and if you have a good set of coals, place the Dutch oven on a grill melt the oil.

Then fry the chopped vegetables, Onions and garlic for about 5 minutes and then add enough water to fill the pot with water about an inch of water.

Cover with the lid and settle in the coals.

Put some coals on top on top of the lid.

Boil the vegetables for about 1 hour, Check carefully regularly to make sure there is still some water in the pot more if necessary until the vegetables are gentle.

When they're done, throw out the rest of the ingredients and let cook a few minutes until everything is warm and combined.

73

VEGETARIAN ITALIAN FRITTATA

INGREDIENTS

- 2 medium-sized mushrooms
- 1/2 red pepper
- 1/2 onion
- 1 clove of garlic
- 4 eggs
- 100 ml milk
- 2 bay leaves
- 1 tsp dried oregano
- Salt and pepper
- Olive oil

METHOD

Heat the oil in the pan and add in onion, pepper, and mushroom.

Cook up browned, then add the garlic and bay leaves, cook for another minute.

Crack the eggs in a jug and then add the milk.

Oregano and spices. Beat until everything is mixed.

Pour the mixture into the saucepan

Set the heat to the lowest level immediately and put a lid on the pot.

Leave on for 10 to 20 minutes until the mixture has risen put (it shouldn't wobble), then cut into portions!

ABOUT THIS RECIPE

This vegetarian Thai red curry is fragrant and spicy, and it's the perfect recipe to warm you up after a long drink day full of outside activities. This makes a filling meal with naan bread served on the side.

74

THAI RED CURRY WITH HALLOUMI

INGREDIENTS

- 3-4 tablespoons of olive oil
- 1 medium-sized onion, diced
- 2 red peppers; washed, pitted and sliced
- 1/2 glass of Thai red curry paste
- 1 block of halloumi, sliced
- 1 can of chickpeas, drained
- Half a 500 g box of tomato passata
- 1 tbspcornflour combined with 2 tbsp Thicken water if necessary
- Cashew nuts and parsley

METHOD

Heat 2 tablespoons of olive oil in the pan over medium heat.

Roast the peppers and halloumi until the peppers have softened, and the halloumi is golden on both side (turn the halloumi while cooking). Remove that

Put the peppers and the halloumi out of the pan and set aside.

Dice the onion and add another 1-2 tablespoons

Add oil to the pan and let it warm up.

Fry the onion until softened and then add the curry paste and stir well to coat the onions.

Add the chickpeas, coconut milk, and tomato passata

Put in the pan and stir well.

Return the peppers to the pan so that they can soak up the taste of the sauce when cooking.

Let the curry steep for about 15-20 minutes over medium heat.

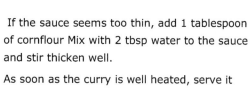

If the sauce seems too thin, add 1 tablespoon of cornflour Mix with 2 tbsp water to the sauce and stir thicken well.

As soon as the curry is well heated, serve it with the fried halloumi on the side (or mix in the sauce if

They prefer).

75

GARAM MASALA SWEET POTATO AND KALE SCRAMBLE

INGREDIENTS

- 2 cups of crushed sweet potatoes
- 1 tbsp dried onion
- 1 tbsp oil (avocado or coconut)
- 5 eggs
- 1 cup of chopped Kale
- 1 tsp Garam Masala spice
- 1 teaspoon of chopped garlic
- 1 / 2½ tsp sea salt
- 1/2 tsp black pepper

METHOD

(AT HOME)

Place the eggs in a bowl and mix in the masala spice, garlic, salt, and pepper.

Store in a small recycled water bottle or another container like a plastic container with a tight lid.

Put the crushed sweet potatoes and onions together in a small plastic bag and chopped Kale in another.

(IN CAMPING)

Heat the cast-iron skillet and oil over medium heat and then add the sweet potato mixture evenly Layer.

Cook for 8-10 minutes or until when the potatoes are starting to soften .

Apply and cover the Kale and egg mixture with foil for a few minutes until the eggs begin to adjust.

Then stir everything and let it cook a few more minutes until the eggs are with you

Taste. Enjoy!

76

VEGAN SWEET POTATO, BLACK BEANS, AND COCONUT CURRY

INGREDIENTS

- *3 large sweet potatoes; diced, skin on*
- *100 g of dried black beans*
- *1 can of full-fat coconut milk*
- *1 small white onion, chopped*
- *1 clove of garlic, crushed*
- *2 chopped lettuce or vine tomatoes*
- *1 sprig of fresh thyme*
- *1/2 tsp paprika, curry powder, Garam Masala & Chili Powder*
- *1/2 tsp black mustard seeds*
- *Season with salt and pepper*
- *1 tablespoon of tasteless cooking oil*
- *2 cups of water*
- *Soy milk (optional)*

METHOD

Soak the black beans in a cup of cold water for at least 2 hours or, if possible overnight.

Simmer gently in a deep non-stick coated saucepan

Let it stand for 25-30 minutes, then drain and let it solidify aside.

In the same pan, heat the oil over low heat.

Add mustard seeds, onion, and garlic and fry until they start popping.

Put the potatoes with the spices in the pan,

Thyme, spice, and a second cup of water.

Steam for 15 minutes with the lid closed until the mixture is soft.

Stir in the chopped tomatoes and black beans and coconut milk.

Let it cook for 5 minutes and remove from the heat.

The sauce should be thick and creamy, coating the back of a spoon.

Drizzle with soy cream and serve with everyone

Cereals or bread for a filling family party!

77

PUMPKIN TAGINE WITH CAULIFLOWER RICE AND HERBY TAHINI DRESSING

INGREDIENTS

- 2 tablespoons of olive oil
- 2 onions, roughly chopped
- 1 tsp cumin
- 1 tsp coriander
- 1 tsp chili flakes
- 1 tsp cinnamon
- 1/2 tsp ground ginger
- 3 cloves of garlic, sliced
- 2 tbsp tomato paste
- 1 small butternut squash
- 1 red pepper sliced
- 2 carrots, cut into pieces
- 1/2 cup of chopped organic apricots
- 1½ + 1/2 pint vegetable broth
- Half a lemon juice
- 1 tsp sea salt
- Some black pepper

METHOD

Pour the olive oil in a large pan and heat to low/medium heat.

Add the chopped onion and fry for 10 minutes soft and browning

Add garlic and spices, stir for a few minutes

Add tomato paste, vegetable broth and apricots, and chopped vegetables.

Approximately Simmer for 20 minutes until the pumpkin is tender.

Add chickpeas, lemon juice, and salt and pepper to season.

Drizzle with tahini

Dressing and coriander & mint.

- *1 can organic chickpeas*
- *Pomegranate seeds (optional)*
- *(pre-made) cauliflower rice*

Tahini dressing

- *A handful of coriander and mint*
- *1 tbsp tahini*
- *1 clove of garlic*
- *Juice from 1 lemon*
- *Sea-salt*
- *Black pepper*
- *Water*

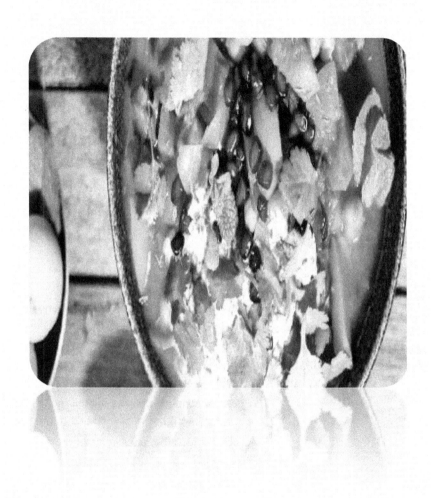

ABOUT THIS RECIPE

Pilafi Pourgouri is a Greek Cypriot dish from Bulgarian wheat that is readily available in Supermarkets in the dried beans and legumes aisle.

78

PILAFI POURGOURI

INGREDIENTS

- Olive oil
- 1 medium white onion, finely chopped
- 4-6 cloves of garlic, finely chopped (depending on taste) their size and how much you like garlic!)
- 30 g spaghetti, broken into small pieces
- 200 g Bulgur wheat
- 1 x 400 g can chop tomatoes
- Hot water
- 2 vegetable stock cubes
- 1 tbsp tomato paste
- Salt

METHOD

Warmth some olive oil in a large, heavy-based saucepan

Gently sweat the oil, then the onions and garlic until they are soft and dry translucent - this takes about 5 minutes.

Stir in the spaghetti and bulgur wheat the onion-garlic mixture.

Add the chopped tomatoes and fill the empty tomato can with hot water and add to the pan.

Crumble the stock cubes and add the tomato Puree. Stir everything well.

Bring to the boil and stir from time to time to prevent the wheat catches on the bottom of the pan.

Take off the stove, cover with a tea towel, and Put the lid on the pan.

Let steam for about 20 minutes.

When the liquid is absorbed, you will know that it is ready, and the Bulgur wheat has softened but still has a little bit on it. You can also add more water if necessary when steaming.

79

STEW PASTA

INGREDIENTS

- *1/2 onion*
- *2 cloves of garlic*
- *2 tbsp chopped basil*
- *1 tablespoon of olive oil*
- *1/2 tsp lemon juice*
- *1 glass of black olives*
- *1/2 glass capers*
- *1 tbsp chopped parsley*
- *500 g spaghetti*
- *350 g tomato sauce*
- *Salt/pepper to taste*

METHOD

Set the olive oil in a large pot and add the onions and garlic and cook until translucent.

Add the remaining ingredients, including the dry spaghetti; otherwise, it wouldn't be a "one pot."

After adding the pasta sauce, refill the sauce

Pour twice with water and add to the pan.

Depending on which pasta you use.

As soon as the pasta softens, stir gently with the ingredients and stir regularly

The pasta is soft, and all ingredients are combined

You may need to add a little more water during this process because the noodles soak up a lot - just make sure there is always some liquid Sauce around the spaghetti.

Take off the stove, with salt & pepper

80

SWEET BEAN CURRY

INGREDIENTS

- 2 cans of red kidney beans or other beans you want to use
- 1 tablespoon of vegetable oil
- 1 apple
- 175 g mushrooms
- 1 tbsp curry powder
- 1 tbsp lemon juice
- 1/2 tsp salt
- 1 tbsp chutney
- 50 g raisins
- 50 g coconut cream

METHOD

Open the beans and let them drain.

Peel, chop, wipe and slice the onion

Cut the mushrooms and apple into small slices

Chop or peel if you like.

Put fruits and vegetables in a large saucepan and fry gently with the oil.

Add the curry powder and hiss a little, then add lemon juice, chutney, salt and raisins, and beans.

Add enough water to wet it and then taste and season if necessary.

Let cook for 10-15 minutes by stirring

Add Coconut cream just before serving!

81

PAELLA WITH SEAFOOD

INGREDIENTS

- 1 tablespoon of olive oil
- 30 g chorizo or summer sausage
- 1 shallot
- 2 tbsp tomato paste (in tubes)
- 1/2 tsp sweet smoked paprika
- 1/2 vegetable stock cubes
- Salt to taste
- 2/3 cup of paella rice
- 1 can of smoked mussels
- 1 can of squid (approx. 100 g) in the ink
- 1 can of shrimp in brine

METHOD

Warmth the olive oil in a pot on medium heat.

Add the finely chopped shallot and cook until shallot is soft and golden.

Add diced chorizo and cook with stirring for 3-4 hours

Stir in the tomato paste and paprika.

 Pour in rice and 2 cups of water. Bring to a boil and crumble in the stock cube.

Season to taste and let warm for about 15 minute.

Stir in the drained seafood and cook for another 5-10 minutes together until the rice is ready, and almost all of the liquid is absorbed.

ABOUT THIS RECIPE

The tasty, garlicky stew of meat and beans requires very little preparation and will continue to cook slowly on the glow of a midday fire. The white beans are light and easy to carry to your camp, but you have to remember to water them at least five hours to get the juicy lipstick texture that you want to dish. Other types of meat can be added to the pot and cooked slowly with everything else. Duck, for example, is fantastic

BONFIRE CASSOULET WITH RAMSON SODA BREAD

INGREDIENTS

CASSOULET

- *400 g of dried white beans*
- *8 pork sausages*
- *500 g boneless*

Cut pork belly into it 1-inch cubes.

- *2 large cloves*

Chopped garlic as small as possible

- *1 large white onion cut thin*
- *Salt and pepper*
- *3 tablespoons of olive oil*

Soda Bread

- *500g flour*
- *2 tsp bicarbonate soda*

METHOD (CASSOULET)

Put the oil in a pan glowing coals, add the cut one Onions and cook for a couple of minutes until translucent (if the pan gets too hot, pull it away from the coals for a bit).

Add the chopped garlic and cook for just a few more minutes.

Now add all the meat and beans and season well.

Cover that mix with water put the lid on and back on the embers

Cook slowly for 2-3 hours, stir very occasionally.

Water may need to be refilled a couple of times to stop that mix of getting too fat, but that's all the stew helps needs. Serve with bread.

METHOD (SODA BREAD)

- 1 tsp salt
- 400 ml live yogurt or buttermilk
- 10 wild leaves chopped garlic of what you want
- Pan
- Wooden spoons

Mix the dry ingredients in a bowl.

Add the yogurt and garlic and bring together

Make a dough. Do not knead the dough.

Oil a Dutch oven.

Put in the dough and press into a bowl level layer.

Score the dough deep (almost cutting) in a cross shape.

Put the lid on the Dutch oven

Hot coals on the edge of your fire.

Pile up even more hot embers on top of the lid. Be very careful to do this!

Approximately bake for 20 minutes

The bread is ready when the stick or knife or sliver of Wood in the loaf, and it comes out clean.

You can do all kinds of flavored bread

Leave out the garlic and add the herbs of your choice.

You could even do a sweet of and Add sugar and chocolate French fries!

If you cook this dish over a fire or on your grill, a little smoky goodness and amaze your friends with your rustic cooking skills. You need a cast-iron Dutch oven for this or a pot that is used forever outside.

83

GRILL BEEF AND PARSNIP STEW

INGREDIENTS

- 1½ pound upper sirloin, cut and trimmed

- ½ inch cubes (with a good cut will last the beef tender. You can use a cheaper one to cut, but you will have to let it simmer Beef longer and need additional inventory crown it with as it boils down)

- 35 g of flour

- 2 tablespoons of olive oil, Divided

- 4 medium-sized carrots, peeled and cut into pieces ½-inch cubes

- 3 small parsnips, peeled and cut into pieces ½-inch cubes

- 450 g starch Potatoes, peeled and cut into ½ inch cubes

METHOD

Arrange your grill for indirect cooking or your fire, so you have a security zone

Reduce the fire if it is too hot. You want a medium heat.

Add a squeeze of salt and pepper to flour.

Throw in beef cubes seasoned flour in a sealable bag.

Shake off the excess flour.

Warmth 1 tablespoon of oil in a large pot with a heavy bottom and fry half of the beef a medium-high heat for 5 Minutes too brown.

Transfer browned beef to a plate and continue cooking remaining beef.

Warmth the remaining oil in the pot and add the carrots, parsnips, Potatoes, onions, garlic, and Fry thyme for 10 minutes at medium heat.

Add browned beef Stock, Stout, and Worcestershire

Put the sauce in the saucepan.

- *1 onion, peeled and diced*
- *1 tablespoon of chopped garlic*
- *2 tbsp fresh thyme leaves*
- *650 ml beef broth*
- *1 can good beer*
- *1 tbsp Worcestershire sauce*
- *1 tbsp cornstarch*
- *Maple syrup*
- *Salt and pepper*
- *BBQ*
- *Ziplock bag*
- *Pot with a strong base*
- *Plate*
- *Fork*

Scape everyone bits from the bottom of the pan to put in the stew

Drizzle with maple syrup and add something sweet and put the Bitterness of the stout to add a little to taste.

Taste and decide if you want some more in it.

Start with about 2 tablespoons.

Simmer over medium heat another 20 minutes or until the vegetables are fork-soft and meat is soft, then season

Season with salt and pepper.

Whisk cornstarch and put the remaining broth in a cup and stir in the stew.

This will thicken it liquid to an almost sauce-like Consistency. Serve hot

ABOUT THIS RECIPE

It is salty and pulls out the excess moisture. The result is a firmer fish that can last up to three years in the marinade in the refrigerator. It's easier to put one on Skewer keeps. There is no need for additional Spice. Most Supermarkets stock the Japanese ingredients.

84

MISO SALMON

INGREDIENTS

- *3 tbsp white miso*
- *2 tbsp mirin (Japanese sweet cooking wine)*
- *1 tablespoon of sugar*
- *1 tbsp sake (Japanese rice wine)*
- *2x 100 g salmon*
- *Knife*
- *Flat dish for marinade and fish*
- *Paper towels*
- *Frying pan*
- *Spatula*
- *Wooden skewers (optional)*

METHOD

Make the marinade by joining all the ingredients except salmon.

Cut the salmon into 2-inch slices.

Let marinate for 30 minutes or overnight, then wipe most

Put the wooden skewers soaked in the marinade on top and fry

Grill or bake in the oven for 15 minutes (skin burns light).

No additional salt is required, but feel free to add some chili if you'd like it hot.

It can be taken hot or cold and is stable for up to three days in the fridge.

Make another meal out of it: Peel off any leftovers and eat them over a bowl of hot, fluffy rice and vegetables of your choice — another all-in-one.

ABOUT THIS RECIPE

Let's talk to the king of the grill. While most people think of burgers and steak is the ideal protein for barbecuing by far the most giving of the animals we feed on. Everyone has a favorite and a specialty that they bring out in society. For this, you need at least 10 to 12 hours, slowly delicious food.

85

SWEET SPICE BBQ PULLED PORK AND COLESLAW

INGREDIENTS

KANSAS CITY RUB

- *3 tbsp smoked paprika*
- *2½ teaspoons freshly ground black pepper*
- *2½ tsp kosher salt*
- *2½ tsp chili powder*
- *2½ tsp granulated garlic*
- *2½ teaspoons of onion powder*
- *½ cup of brown sugar*
- *1 tsp cayenne pepper (less or more to taste and preference) barbecue sauce*
- *4 tablespoons of butter*
- *1 small red onion, finely chopped*
- *4 cloves of garlic, finely chopped*

METHOD (RUB & SAUCE)

Melt the butter in medium volume

Pot over medium-high heat.

Add chopped onion and cook until they're translucent, then type that

Cook garlic and cook for 30 seconds.

Add ketchup, molasses, brown sugar, vinegar, mustard, chili powder, black pepper, and Cayenne pepper with onions and garlic and stir.

Bring to a boil and reduce to warm for 30 minutes, stirring frequently.

Put sauce in blender or Food Processor and mix up smooth.

Let cool down and a storable glass. It will stay that way a month in the fridge.

METHOD (PULLED PORK)

Now set up your barbecue area one side lit and the other Page out. You don't want to heat

- *560 ml ketchup*
- *115 g molasses*
- *55 g of dark brown sugar*
- *75 ml of cider vinegar*
- *2 tbsp squeezable yellow mustard*
- *1 tablespoon of chili powder*
- *1 tsp freshly ground black pepper*
- *½ teaspoon cayenne pepper*

Pepper (optional)

COLESLAW

- *½ head green Cabbage, shredded*
- *2 carrots, grated*
- *1 red onion, thin sliced*
- *2 green onions, chopped*
- *350 g mayonnaise*
- *62 g Dijon mustard*
- *1 tbsp apple cider vinegar*
- *1 lemon, juiced*
- *Pinch of sugar*
- *Kosher salt and freshly ground black pepper*

TENSIONED PIG

- *Pork shoulder*
- *BBQ*
- *Wood chips*
- *Foil*
- *Pan*
- *Two forks*
- *Apple juice / cider (Optional)*
- *Middle pot*
- *Mixer/food processor*

under the meat. Stop a constant temperature of 121C and prepare your wood chips.

Take a handful dry

French fries and put them on a sheet from foil. Plus a handful of chips that you have soaked for at least an hour

Water or even cider if you want to Get in the mood.

Roll up the fries, stab into a tree trunk, and pierce the foil with a knife, so the smoke is the place to flee.

Do three, or you can replace 4 of them exhaust them as they do.

The drought Wood will smoke quickly, and that wet will smolder and give you one longer smoking time.

The grill is now ready Pork is grated and has been added

Room temperature for around 20 minutes and smoke is billowing out.

Place your shoulder on a rack, an aluminum pan.

Pour some Apple juice or cider on it.

Then place the bottom of the pan with the shoulder on the indirect side of the grill away from the direct heat under.

Place the smoke pack (wood chips Packages) on or near the heat Element so they can smoke away and hug your pork Shoulder.

Open a beer and relax.

Your only job now is to do it

Make sure the grill stays on you

Constant 121C for the next 10 to 12 hours.

When you see the smoke stopped, replace the smoke pack and add a little more liquid (Juice or cider) on the floor of the pan.

- *Jug*
- *2 large bowls*
- *Knife*
- *Cling film*

Turn your shoulder so that all sides have a chance to be near and far heated side.

Look for an internal Temperature of 93 ° C.

Once you reach this point, take the shoulder off, wrap it with foil and let it rest for 20 minutes.

This is when the juices redistribute over the shoulder.

When you're done, use two Forks to chop the meat.

If it has to be cut, then you took it out too early. It is extreme hard-to-boil pulled pork.

Mix the crushed loveliness with some BBQ sauce - just enough to wet it.

You can always add later if you have to.

Serve with fresh rolls crispy coleslaw on and drizzled with a sweet BBQ sauce.

ABOUT THIS RECIPE

Sometimes you just need a good meal to finish eating Day - and this recipe makes it perfect. The couscous fills up as the whiskey sets fire to your stomach and holds the warm-up on a cool evening.

86

WHISKEY MEATBALLS

INGREDIENTS

- *A pack of 20 ready-made meatballs*
- *120 ml ketchup*
- *85 g of brown sugar*
- *60 ml bourbon whiskey*
- *1 teaspoon of fresh lemon juice*
- *1 tsp Worcestershire sauce*
- *1 pepper*
- *2 large carrots*
- *2 small red onions*
- *1 zucchini*
- *240 g couscous*
- *Cast iron pot and stainless steel pot*
- *Wooden spoons*
- *Knife*
- *Peeler*
- *chopping board*
- *Plastic bowl and plate*
- *baking gloves*

METHOD

Add the whiskey, ketchup, brown sugar, Worcestershire, and lemon juice sauce in one large cast-iron saucepan and mix well.

Stir in the meatballs sure they are all well covered the whiskey sauce.

Find 4 flat stones and place them in a place next to the fire,

Leave gaps between the rocks.

Check the pot balance well on the rocks, and scoop carefully glows through the gaps.

Put your pot on the hot rocks

Cover and let it steep simmer for about an hour, stir a few times.

Make Sure the dish doesn't cook too vigorously; otherwise, you will burn all this beautiful whiskey!

In the meantime, peel and chop carrots, onions, and the rest of the vegetables.

Once an hour has passed, add Put them in the pot, stir and cover again for half an hour.

When the food bubbles too much, gently move the pot a little further away from the fire.

Fill a medium-sized stainless steel

Cover steel pot with water place a lid and near the fire.

Let it cook for a few minute.

Place the couscous in a plastic bowl and pour in the boiling water, and then with a Plate.

The water should be twice the amount

Put the couscous in the bowl.

Then cover and go.

This should take 5-7 minutes to Cook.

Once your whiskey meatballs are cooked, and the couscous is done, carefully in spoon Bowls and enjoy!

This is a very simple and great little camping recipe with a nifty trick for making the hot dogs. Simple, cheap, tasty, and hardly rinses.

87

CAMPFIRE HOT DOGS & CRISPY BREAD

INGREDIENTS:

- sausages
- Ketchup
- Crispy baguette
- beans
- Marshmallows

WHAT YOU WILL NEED:

- metal skewers
- Campfire
- Refractory saucepan or saucepan

METHOD

The trick is to pre-cook the sausages at home when you have your campfire all you have to do is hold on to them on some metal skewers and brown them round off the edges with the flames (rather as they cook all the way through)

Once the sausages look flame-roasted, could you put them in a piece of crispy bread?

A little ketchup and you're good to go

Usually, open a tin of beans if we fancy a side dish.

Either cook in a saucepan on the fire or heat with a small gas stove

Roast a few marshmallows for dessert your metal skewers over the embers of the campfire before going to bed!

88

QUICK AND EASY COWBOY BEANS

INGREDIENTS:

- *2 x 400 g cans of baked beans in tomato sauce*
- *1 x 400 g can of red kidney beans, drained and rinsed*
- *1 red onion, finely chopped*
- *½ tsp garlic salt*
- *2-4 tablespoons grill sauce*
- *Spray on oil*

WHAT YOU WILL NEED:

- *Cooking pot*

METHOD:

Spray some oil in a saucepan and sweat the onions until they are tender. Scatter the garlic salt over the onions

Put the beans in the pan and stir in some barbecue sauce - you can do this to taste

Heat and serve the beans!

Goes well with burgers, hot dogs and in baked potatoes

89

HONEY MUSTARD CHICKEN

INGREDIENTS:

- 4 tablespoons butter, melted
- 2 tbsp liquid honey
- 2 tablespoons of Dijon mustard
- 1 tbsp Montreal chicken spice (see below)
- 4 boneless, skinless chicken breasts, trimmed
- 2 large sweet potatoes, decorticate and cut in ¾ inch cubes
- ½ large sweet red pepper, trimmed and cut into 1 inch pieces
- 2 spring onions, cut and cut

Montreal Chicken Seasoning:

- 4 tablespoons of fine sea salt
- 1 tbsp black pepper
- 1 tablespoon of onion powder (not salt)
- ½ tablespoon of garlic powder (not salt)
- ½ tbsp crushed red chili flakes (or to taste)

METHOD:

Cut 4 large pieces of aluminum foil

Place the potatoes in a microwave bowl, then cook them high for 5-7 minutes, stirring every 2 minutes until soft

Divide the potatoes, peppers and chicken breast over the 4 foil pieces

Whisk butter, honey, mustard, and chicken and pour an equal amount over the servings

Bring up two inverse sides of the foil to hit and cover the chicken and vegetables. Fold tight and leave room for expansion. Seal the ends

Place on a grill that you have heated on medium heat. Cover with a metal lid (Make sure it has a heat-resistant handle)

Grill for 18-20 minutes, turning the chicken every 10 minutes. It will be ready when the juices are clear

Pull back the film and cover each with some spring onions and Serve

- ½ tbsp dried thyme

- ½ tbsp dried rosemary

- ½ tbsp coriander seeds, crushed

WHAT YOU WILL NEED:

- Knife

- Foil

- bowl

- Whisk

- Fork

- spoons

- Frying pan/grill

90

HUNTER'S CHICKEN FOIL PACKS

INGREDIENTS:

- 500 g baked potatoes, peeled and cut into inch cubes
- 1 tbsp Italian herb and garlic spice
- Season with salt and pepper
- 2 teaspoons of oil
- 4 boneless, breastless chicken breast fillets, cut off
- 1½ teaspoons of grill spice (see below)
- 4 slices of bacon strips, cooked and halved
- 120 g grated cheddar cheese
- 60 g BBQ sauce
- 2 chopped spring onions

BBQ SEASONS:

- ½ tbsp dried thyme
- 1 tablespoon of garlic powder
- 1 tbsp dried parsley flakes
- ½ tsp celery salt

METHOD:

Tear off 4 large pieces of high-performance aluminum foil

Put the potatoes in a bowl together with the oil, the Italian herbs and the garlic season and season with salt and black pepper

Season the chicken with the grilling spice and place 1 piece of the chicken in the middle of each piece of foil

Spread the potatoes evenly and place them on the foil around the chicken.

Place slices of bacon over the chicken

Bring up two faces of the foil to meet over the chicken. Seal edges make a ½ inch fold to allow expansion. Fold in the other seal edges

Place on a grill over medium heat. Cover with a metal lid. Cooking for 18-20 minutes, turn the packs half a turn every 10 minutes. When the chicken is ready, the juices will run clear.

Tear open the top. Sprinkle part of the cheese over the glass potatoes in every pack. Spread 1/4 of the BBQ sauce at the top of each piece of chicken, garnish with the spring onions and serve

- *2 tsp mild chili powder*
- *½ tablespoon of garlic powder (not salt)*
- *½ tbsp black pepper*
- *60 g of fine sea salt*
- *½ tablespoon of ground cumin*
- *1 tablespoon of onion powder (not salt)*
- *2 tablespoons of dried mustard powder*
- *1 tsp cayenne pepper (or to taste)*
- *75 g soft light brown sugar*

WHAT YOU WILL NEED:
- *Knife*
- *Foil*
- *bowl*
- *Fork*
- *spoons*
- *Frying pan/grill*

91

RAGU LENTILS WITH SPAGHETTI

INGREDIENTS:

- 320 g whole grain spaghetti
- 1 tablespoon of olive oil
- 1 large onion, finely chopped
- 225 g red lentils
- 3 tbsp tomato paste
- 2 teaspoons of garlic granules
- 575 ml of boiling water
- 100 g grated cheddar
- 1 tsp salt, ½ tsp pepper

WHAT YOU WILL NEED:

- chopping board
- Sharp knife
- 2 pots
- Digital scales
- A spoon (to stir the mixture)

METHOD:

Fry the onion in olive oil until cooked

Add the boiling water garlic granules, lentils, and Tomato puree.

Simmer very gently with the lid closed about 20 minutes. Stirring occasionally again and keep it in mind as the mixture can stick if the water is absorbed.

If it looks too dry, add a shot more water

Add salt and pepper. Try and add more if necessary

Cook the spaghetti in salted water until tender when the lentils are cooking.

Drain well

Stir about half of the ragus through the spaghetti and put the spaghetti in heated bowls. Top with the rest Ragu, then the grated cheese

Serve with salad if desired

Preparation for this recipe can be started at home, and you can take the finished burgers with you in a cool box.

92

MEDITERRANEAN FALAFEL BURGER

INGREDIENTS:

- Drain 400 g can of chickpeas
- 2 tablespoons of olive cubes or dried tomatoes
- 1 tsp garlic paste
- 1 tbsp chopped basil
- 1 slice of bread, grated to form breadcrumbs
- Season with salt and pepper

WHAT YOU WILL NEED:

- bowl
- Hand blender/potato masher
- BBQ grill / pan

METHOD:

Children can help you place the ingredients in a bowl wort

Roughly stir with a hand blender (if you want to make this recipe while out camping, you could mash the ingredients together with a potato masher)

Children can help to form the mixture into burger shapes with their hands. Use one little flour to dust your hands and the outside of the burger when the mixture is too sticky

Brush the burgers before cooking with a little oil. Place on the grill or in a frying pan on a gas stove. Cook for 5 minutes on each side until golden

ABOUT THIS RECIPE

Most kids love pizza. These pocket pizzas are easy, quick to prepare, and best of all, you can get the kids involved with creating them. They cook around the campfire and can also be cooked on hot coals.

93

POCKET PIZZAS

INGREDIENTS:

• A packet of pita bread

• Can or glass of spaghetti or pizza sauce

• Grated cheese

• Optional fillings: sweet corn, pineapple pieces, Pepper cubes etc.

• Foil

* Please note that these pizzas are roasted so that you can

Need to choose fillings that can be eaten raw (i.e. used cooked meat)
*

What you will need:

• Knife

• spoons

• Foil

• Campfire

METHOD:

First, cut each flatbread in half bag format

Pour a spoon of pizza sauce - try and spread it evenly in your pocket

Add fillings and cover with the grid cheese. Do not overfill the flatbread!

Carefully wrap the flatbread in foil and over the hot coals of a campfire or hung over the fire

The cooking time depends on your fire; as a rough idea, you need 2 minutes on each side of the pizza. Best to check the first pizza after a minute unpack to see how it works and judge for yourself

The pocket pizza should be a flatbread

This is not burned with the heated sauce through and the cheese melted

Time to enjoy your pizzas around the clock Campfire!

TOP:

* If you find that your pizza bread is sticking to the foil, you might want to grease it first and further away from the heat*

94

SWEET AND SOUR CHICKEN

INGREDIENTS:

- *4 boneless and skinless chicken breasts, cut off of any fat*
- *Seasoned salt*
- *8 tbsp finely chopped orange jam*
- *3 tbsp sweet chili sauce*
- *3 tbsp rice wine vinegar*
- *1 small red and one green pepper, cut into stripes*
- *1 x 425 g pieces of pineapple in a can, drained*
- *High-performance aluminum foil*

What you will need:

- *Knife*
- *Foil*
- *bowl*
- *Fork/whisk*
- *spoons*
- *Frying pan/grill*

METHOD:

Cut 4 large rectangular pieces of film

Whisk the jam, sweet chili sauce, and rice wine vinegar. To adjust aside. Prepare your vegetables

3. Season the chicken with seasoning salt and add a piece to the pan

Middle of each square slide

Pour 1 tablespoon of jam over each Mix and ¼ of the pineapple and Pepper slices. Share the rest of the sauce between them all

Fold the foil over the chicken and vegetables so that the edges meet in the

Center. Seal it tightly and make a ½ inch crease.

Seal the ends and leave room for expansion

Heat up the BBQ grill. Put the packages on the grill on medium heat. Cover with a metal lid (make sure it's heat-resistant Stud)

Let it cook for 20 to 30 minutes, rotating the packages every 10 minutes or so. When done, the chicken juices run clear

Cut an X over each package and serve with some steamed rice

95

ZESTY LEMON SPAGHETTI

INGREDIENTS:

- 1 tablespoon of olive oil
- 2 carrots
- 1 leek
- 750 g ground beef
- 500 ml stock
- 1 lemon with zest
- Spaghetti

What you will need:

- Stove
- Knife

METHOD:

Halve the flatbread and pizza

Cut the topping into bite-size pieces if necessary

Warm the pizza sauce and toppings in the pan

Pot on a camping stove for about 5 minutes

Add the cheese to the pizza sauce and stir to integrate

Fill or put a flatbread bag mix on a flatbread and enjoy your meal!

This is a considerable recipe for using leftovers throughout Camping (or at home!) Offers spring Onions, vegetarian sausages, tomatoes, and vegans Cheese. Of course, you can also use meat sausages and milk cheese and any vegetables of your choice.

96

FOLDED QUESADILLAS

INGREDIENTS:

- 2 tortilla wraps
- 3 chopped spring onions
- 1 chopped tomato
- 2 chopped vegetarian sausages
- Grate some cheese
- 4 beaten eggs
- olive oil

What you will need:

- Knife
- Fork
- frying pan
- spoons

METHOD:

Chop the sausages into 1 cm slices

Cut onions and tomatoes

Beat the eggs

Put some oil in a pan and heat medium

Add the sausages and cook until they are brown

Add the vegetables and continue cooking until softens

Add the egg and stir with the vegetables to your desired consistency

Spread the egg and vegetables evenly in the middle of the two tortilla wraps and sprinkle with a little cheese

Fold one edge of the wrapper toward middle and keep going until the middle is covered (five-folds around the mixture is what it takes)

Clean the pan with a cloth and add a little more oil

Add one of the folded quesadillas and fold the page down and fry until they're brown

Turn and repeat on the sealed side

Repeat with the second

Enjoy with a bit of sauce

SNACKS

Dessert couldn't be easier.

You can enjoy this cold or warm-up over the grill!

97

OLIVE OIL & SEA SALT DATES

INGREDIENTS

- ½ cup of Medjool appointments
- 1 tablespoon of olive oil
- Sea-salt

METHOD

Dust sea salt and olive oil on the dates and enjoy or first heat the dates and olive oil in a small pan sprinkle with sea salt.

ABOUT THIS RECIPE

A fruity, sweet, and spicy drink, like a slush for adults. Blackberries and sorrel are both very common wild ingredients that you can find yourself.

Fresh and free!

98

BLACKBERRY & SORREL CRUSH

INGREDIENTS

- *A small handful of blackberries*
- *6 large common sorrel leaves*
- *Basil branch*
- *vodka*
- *Sugar*
- *Lemonade*
- *Ice*

What you will need

Glass

Rolling pin (or camping racket handle)

METHOD

Mix the fruits and sorrel with a stable glass and sugar together.

Add vodka and crushed ice, mix more.

Add the soda, stir, and serve.

ABOUT THIS RECIPE

We all need a natural boost of energy when we're on the go.

This decadent mug of hot chocolate tastes indulgent, but it contains everything natural ingredients and is full of nutrients. Cocoa can be quite a powerful stimulant.

99

RAW HOT CHOCOLATE

INGREDIENTS

- 1 cup of milk of your choice
- 2 tsp raw cocoa/cocoa powder
- 1 tsp coconut sugar
- A dash of cinnamon

What you will need

cup

mixer

Small pot

METHOD

Add milk and cocoa powder

Pot and heat gently until the cocoa has dissolved. If you have a blender, you can conjure them up first and then heat in the pan.

If the milk is hot but not boiling, add and mix in the coconut sugar and cinnamon.

Serve immediately in the cup.

ABOUT THIS RECIPE

These raw brownies are a real treat! Sticky, chocolatey, and moreish.

It is unbelievable that they are made from just three ingredients.

After placing them in the freezer, keep them in your cool box, nutritious and energizing snack.

100

RAW CHOCOLATE & HAZELNUT BROWNIES

INGREDIENTS

- *400 g of Medjool dates*
- *150 g roasted hazelnuts without shell*
- *3 tbsp raw cocoa powder (or cocoa powder)*

What you will need

food processor

Square brownie tray

METHOD

Add the hazelnuts in the food processor and grind in a flour.

Add dates and cocoa powder and mix well until a sticky, chocolatey dough forms. You may have to stop a few times to scrape the mixture in the middle.

Squeeze the mixture evenly into a square brownie and put it in the freezer for about an hour or until the brownie batter has consolidated.

Cut into squares or rectangles, wrap greaseproof store paper, and in an airtight container, preferably chilled.

ABOUT THIS RECIPE

The Acai Berry and Chia Seed Pudding is a perfect kick start meal anyone's morning. Not only does it take little time to prepare, It only contains a few ingredients, which is perfect if you are camping. Chia seeds and acai are also packaged with nutrients, protein, and a lot of goodness; therefore, you will be left feeling healthy and energized.

101

ACAI FRUIT & CHIA SEED PUDDING

INGREDIENTS

- ½ cup of whole chia seeds
- 2 cups of milk, soy milk or vegetable milk
- 2 tbsp maple syrup
- 1 tsp acai powder
- Handful of blueberries

METHOD

Mix milk, chia seeds, and maple syrup and put the acai powder in a bowl until everything is well mixed.

Cover the bowl or pour the mixture in two jam jars and in the fridge or cool box overnight (or for at least 4 hours).

Wake up, take your jam jar, and before you eat sprinkle blueberries over it.

You can differentiate your recipe by adding different one's flavors like cocoa with pudding as well as an addition of various toppings such as bananas.

Still hungry after dinner? This recipe is the perfect one dessert to fill you with delicious goodness. And only that takes 5 minutes to make!

102

ARROZ CON LECHE – RICE PUDDING

INGREDIENTS

- *75 g instant rice*
- *30 g milk powder (I use coconut)*
- *¼ tsp cinnamon*
- *¼ tsp nutmeg*
- *½ teaspoon of sugar*
- *Raisins*
- *nuts*
- *Grated coconut*
- *Dried apples*

what you will need

- *Ziplock bag*
- *bowl*
- *spoons*

METHOD

Gather all the ingredients in a ziplock bag. If you want to be able to add hot water to the bag instead of using a bowl, use a Freezer ziplock bag.

At Camp

You can ingest this dish hot or cold. For hot, pour 160 ml of hot water over the mixture and let it rest for 5 minutes until the rice is tender. For cold, pour 160ml cold water over the mix an hour or so before wanting to eat and leave until rice is soft.

If you want to be away for several hours, you need some food to maintain your energy level up - and we can't think of a better way to do that than with these delicious coconut almond cookies.

103

NO BAKE COCONUT ALMOND TRAIL COOKIES

INGREDIENTS

- 2 tbsp almond meal
- 25 g of peeled hemp seeds
- 140 g of oatmeal
- 1/8 tsp ground cardamom
- Pinch of salt
- 100 g coconut sugar
- 2 tbsp light coconut milk
- 2 tbsp coconut oil, melted
- 75 g almond butter
- 28 g dark chocolate, cut into pieces

what you will need

- Small bowl
- Small pan
- spoons
- Plate
- Ziplock bag

METHOD

All dry ingredients (hemp seeds, almond flour, cardamom, oatmeal, and salt) in a small bowl and set aside.

Warmth coconut oil, coconut sugar, and coconut milk in a pan over medium heat and bring to a boil for 2 minutes. The mix should be thick and thread-like.

Put the almond butter in the pan and stir until smooth, then remove from the heat. Add the dry ingredients and whisk until evenly coated.

Take a spoonful of dough and roll it until it forms a spherical shape.

Place on a plate and press down so that it looks like a biscuit. Keep doing this with the remainder of the dough, then press the chocolate chunks into the top of each.

Set aside and allow to set (approx. 30 minutes).

Then you can put them in your ziplock bag and take them with you.

If you fancy something sweet, you can't go wrong with this recipe. It is recommended as a dessert but could also be easily eaten as a quick snack.

104

STICKY SWEET PINEAPPLE

INGREDIENTS

- 1 large pineapple (cut into wedges)
- 170 g brown sugar
- 2 tsp cinnamon

What you will need

- bowl
- Freeze bag
- Foil
- BBQ

METHOD

Mix the brown sugar and cinnamon in a small bowl.

Place the sugar-containing mixture in a large freezer bag and add the pineapple wedges in your pocket.

Keep the top of the bag tightly closed and shake the bag around the sugar and cinnamon stick to all sides of the pineapple wedges. Once the whole pineapple is evenly coated, place the pineapple wedges on film and make a film package.

Place the foil box on the grill for 10-15 minutes, and you're ready to enjoy this delicious pleasure!

105

VERY BERRY NO BAKE CRUMBLE

INGREDIENTS

- 175 g freshly picked wild berries (blueberries,

Raspberries, blackberries)

- 1 tablespoon of sugar or to taste

- 70 g crispy muesli

What you will need

- Pan

- spoons

METHOD

Pour the wild berries into the pan and sprinkle them with sugar.

Lead the pan to a boil over medium heat and stir continuously to thick.

Take the pan off the heat and let it cool (5 minutes).

Pour muesli over the berry mixture and enjoy!

This delicious and impressive dessert takes less than 10 minutes to prepare.

Dead easy!

106

BANOFFEE PIE

INGREDIENTS:

• *A pack of cookies of your choice*

• *Butter or margarine*

• *1 can of caramel dessert*

• *1 chopped banana*

• *1 can of whipped cream*

• *1 chocolate flake*

• *Containers to layer the cake (we used drinking glasses as they were handy and the cake looked appetizing in them)*

What you will need:

• *plastic bag (for crushing biscuits)*

• *container (to melt the butter)*

• *spoons*

METHOD:

Crush enough cookies in a bag to cover the base of as many camping glasses as you need

Use half the weight in butter cookies you used. Either melt in a container in the sun or over a campfire

Mix cookies and butter and press into a solid layer in the base of the glasses

Open the can of caramel dessert and add a layer on the biscuit layer. Add in layer chopped banana too

Spray a layer of cream on top and sprinkle on top with pieces of the broken flake

ABOUT THIS RECIPE

Making a campfire can be hard work, and everyone enjoys it. Watch the fire glow and chat friends while making your own bread and chocolate snack.

107

WHITE CHOCOLATE JARS

INGREDIENTS:

- *1 packet of basic pizza mix with added water*
- *Water*
- *1 packet of white chocolate buttons*

What you will need:

- *Bucket of water (keep your hand straight when you burn yourself)*
- *bowl*
- *spoons*
- *Greenstick*
- *penknife*

Serving tips:

- *Make sure before you start cooking your fire area is certain that you are not going falling over anything and that bucket of water is near enough to reach*

METHOD:

Read the instructions on your pizza dough package and make the dough

Crush the dough with your hands until it is stretchy. Take a small serving batter, roll it into a sausage and wrap the sausage around the green stick in a spiral

Make sure you sit quietly and hold your stick and batter over the fire where the embers glow. You will know your damper is cooked when the outside is golden brown, and the inside is fluffy

Inflate the cooked steamer until it is cool enough to touch and then take it from the end of your stick - it should smell delicious!

Take two white chocolate buttons and slide it into the hole on the left in the damper by the stick. Watch the chocolate buttons melt and try not to get white chocolate all over your face while you eat your white chocolate damper!

108

ROCKY ROAD

INGREDIENTS:

- *100 g Maltese*
- *200 g dark chocolate*
- *70 g butter*
- *6 digestive cookies*
- *50 g marshmallows*
- *2 tbsp honey (optional)*

What you will need:

- *bowl*
- *sandwich bag*
- *spatula*
- *Foil*
- *Tray / plastic container*
- *Knife*

METHOD:

Let chocolate, honey, and butter melt a slight heat

Set aside to cool

Bash up the cookies in a sandwich bag until it's a mix of pieces and powder

Add the shredded cookies and marshmallows and Maltese to the mix and gently fold until all ingredients are covered chocolate

Fill in a foil-lined bowl or plastic container. Push the mixture down and pop in the fridge or cool box and leave to set for around 60 minutes

Slice and serve

109

CINNAMON BAKED APPLE

INGREDIENTS:

- apples
- Butter or coconut oil
- almond slices (or a nut of your choice)
- cinnamon
- Raisins
- Grated coconut

What you will need:

- Knife
- spoons
- Oven glove
- High-performance film
- Campfire with coals

METHOD:

Carefully remove the top of each apple to make a lid

Then cut out the core with a spoon and a place for the rubbers

Fill the hole with a piece of butter or add coconut oil and then the coconut and raisins and nuts before sprinkling cinnamon on it above

Wrap the film and place it next to the coals. Let it cook for 20-30 minutes to soft (depending on the size of the apples)

110

SUNNY FRUIT & MARSHMALLOW KABOBS

INGREDIENTS:

- *fruit cubes (melon, pineapple, strawberries)*
- *Marshmallows*

What you will need:

- *wooden skewers*
- *Campfire*

METHOD:

Cut the fruits into bite-sized pieces at home and keep in an airtight container

At camp, slide the fruit onto the grilling sticks alternating with the marshmallows

Use wooden skewers or soaked in water or grill the sticks and roast them over the campfire until the marshmallows are roasted, and the fruit is warm.

111

HORSERADISH MUSHROOM JERKY

INGREDIENTS

- *453 g portobello mushrooms*
- *2 tbsp apple cider vinegar*
- *3 tbsp coconut aminos (or soy sauce)*
- *4 tsp prepared horseradish*
- *½ tsp sea salt*
- *½ teaspoon of garlic powder*

What you will need

knife

4L sealable food bag

dehydrator

METHOD

Cut the mushrooms into strips about 6 cm wide. Mix everything together

Mix well with the remaining ingredients and add to a 4L sealable grocery bag or another sealable container with the mushrooms.

Let marinate overnight until the mushrooms are saturated.

Lie on open racks in your dehydrator for 5-6 hours until dry and tough.

Keep in an airtight container for 4 servings.

ABOUT THIS RECIPE

This is a great way to enjoy beanless hummus and add a little more vitamins and fiber to your diet. Enjoy with sliced vegetables or on your favorite sandwich. Make it at home and store it in a plastic container for your next outdoor adventure.

112

PUMPKIN HUMMUS

INGREDIENTS

- *425 g canned pumpkin*
- *½ cup of tahini*
- *¼ cup of olive oil*
- *Juiced ½ lemon*
- *½ tbsp cumin*
- *½ tbsp of chopped garlic*
- *½ tbsp dried oregano*
- *½ tsp sea salt*

What you will need

Mixing bowl

spoon

Knife (for lemon slicing)

Food processor optional

METHOD

Combine all the ingredients with your hand or in a bowl

Stir the food processor until smooth.

113

MUSSELS

INGREDIENTS

- 1 tsp olive oil
- 2 cloves of garlic - finely chopped
- 1 large onion - chopped
- 900 g mussels
- 230 ml dry white wine
- 150 ml double cream
- Crispy bread to serve

What you will need

dulcimer

knife

frying pan

camping stove

METHOD

If you cook on a camping stove, you want to choose something that can all be done in one pan. This easy mussels recipe is perfect for that. Heat the olive oil in a large saucepan over medium heat. Add in the onion and garlic, then fry for 5 minutes until tender. Add the mussels, the wine and cream, stir and cover the pot. Let cook for 10-15 minutes until the mussels are cooked through. Serve in a bowl with some crispy bread.

This recipe is so easy to cook, and you can add it perfectly to your camping trip. With just simple ingredients, it offers a lot of sweet as usual jam, but with the energizing boost of chia seeds and without all the added sugar.

114

RAW RASPBERRY CHIA JAM

INGREDIENTS

- *2 cups of raspberries*
- *2 tbsp chia seeds*
- *2 tbsp maple syrup*
- *2 tablespoons of warm water*

What you will need

Bowl & fork

Airtight vessel or container

METHOD

Break the raspberries in a bowl with a fork until they become a mushy mixture.

Join in the water, chia seeds, maple syrup, and mix well.

Pour the dough in a container and keep it in the refrigerator to solidify for at least an hour.

Enjoy drizzled over yogurt.

115

SIMPLE SMOKEY BAKED BEANS

INGREDIENTS

- *2 tablespoons of olive oil*
- *1 onion - diced*
- *4 cloves of garlic*
- *1 tsp smoked paprika*
- *½ teaspoon cayenne pepper*
- *1 tsp cumin*
- *2 packs/cans of organic tomatoes*
- *1 zucchini sliced*
- *3 dried tomatoes, chopped fine up (optional)*
- *2 tsp tamari*
- *1 pack of organic borlotti beans*
- *1 pack of organically grown red beans*
- *1 pack of organic cannellini beans*
- *Salt*
- *Pepper*
- *1 tbsp maple syrup*
- *1 tsp apple cider vinegar*

METHOD

Put the onion with the oil in a large pan and fry for 10 minutes over low heat. Put spices and garlic and fry for a few more minutes.

Next, add the zucchini, tomato, and sun-dried tomatoes and simmer for 30 minutes on very low heat.

Finally, add the beans, tamari, maple syrup, apple cider vinegar, liquid smoke, and let simmer for a few minutes, then season with the salt, pepper, and chili to taste.

- *1 tsp liquid smoke (optional)*
- *Optional - sprinkle additionally*

Chili flakes

116

PUFFED QUINOA & PEANUT BUTTER BAR

INGREDIENTS

- 1 cup of dried dates
- 1 cup of puffed quinoa
- ⅓ cup of peeled pumpkin seeds
- ⅓ cup of peeled sunflower seeds, unsalted
- 1 cup of creamy peanut butter
- 2 tbsp coconut oil - melted
- 1 bar (approx. 100 g) dark

Broken chocolate (70% cocoa) in pieces

- ⅓ cup unsweetened desiccated coconut

METHOD

Insert a 25 x 20 cm (8 x 10 ") baking dish parchment paper. Pulse dates in a blender until you get a sticky paste.

Pour the date paste into a large bowl.

Add puffed quinoa, seeds, peanut butter, and coconut oil. Stir until everything is well mixed.

Press into the prepared baking dish the quinoa and peanut butter mixture

Allow the chocolate to melt and spread evenly. Dust with coconut flakes.

Let it cold to room temperature, then store in the refrigerator 2 hours or until firm. Take out the plate from the baking dish and cut it into 12 bars.

Wrap each bar in wax paper or aluminum foil.

Store bars in a closed container in the refrigerator until you are ready to put them in your backpack.

117

SORREL DROP SCONES

INGREDIENTS

- *110 g of gluten-free flour*
- *25 g powdered sugar*
- *1 egg*
- *150 ml milk (full fat)*
- *1 handful of chopped sorrel leaves.*

If you can't find sorrel, use one Elderberries or blueberries

METHOD

Put the flour and sugar in a bowl and mix. Make a fountain in the middle of the mixture and add the egg and half of the milk.

Mix to a dough. Now mix in the rest of the milk. Add the sorrel leaves and stir in.

Heat a flat frying pan or a heavy saucepan until hot grease with lard. Put the dessert spoon of the dough on the dough pan. Leave room for it to spread.

Cook until the air bubbles rise, then turn and cook for about 1 minute more. Place on a cooling shelf and cover.

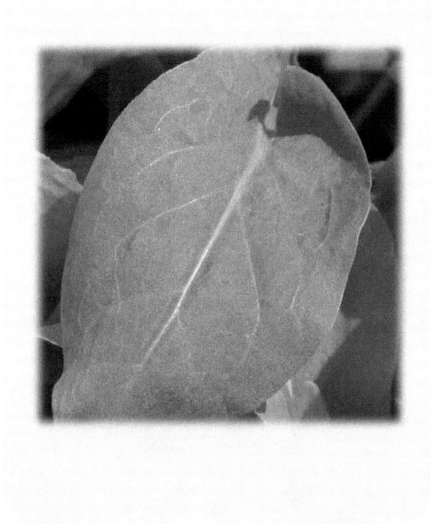

The smokiness of the campfire contributes to the authenticity of the aroma in this simple and delicious bath.

118

CAMPFIRE BABA GANOUSH

INGREDIENTS

- 5 eggplants
- 100 g light tahini paste
- 3 tablespoons of olive oil
- Juice from 1 lemon
- 10-15 wild garlic leaves
-

METHOD

Fry the eggplants directly on the hot coals at the side of the fire until soft and slightly charred.

Let cool marginally, cut in half, and scrape off from the meat in a bowl. Add all the other ingredients to the bowl, season with salt and pepper, and porridge into a coarse paste.

Try and season with salt, pepper, and lemon juice if necessary.

ABOUT THIS RECIPE

These vegan grilled beans are the perfect camping food, a great balance of protein and carbohydrates, and absolutely delicious. They have a really deep, rich taste that's about a billion times tastier than anything you'll ever get from a can, and it's really easy to do on a camping stove.

119

BAKED VEGAN BBQ BEANS

INGREDIENTS

- *400 g canned borlotti beans*
- *1 red onion - diced*
- *500 g tomato passata*
- *1 tbsp tomato paste*
- *1 heaped tsp miso*
- *1 tablespoon of nutritional yeast*
- *1½ tsp hot peppers*
- *1½ teaspoons of dried oregano*
- *A handful of fresh coriander - chopped*

METHOD

Add all ingredients except the coriander, stir well in the pan, bring to the boil then reduce to a simmer

Whisk now and again until all of the luscious flavors have blended together. They're ready to eat as soon as they're heated through thoroughly. The taste gets even richer the longer you cook them for.

Serve with wholemeal or rye toast and sprinkle over it the chopped coriander.

120

CARNE ASADA GARLIC FRIES "VENISON STYLE"

INGREDIENTS

CARNE ASADA

- *2 pounds of wild flank or Rock steak trimmed*
- *½ red onion, sliced*
- *2 limes, juiced*
- *4 cloves of garlic*
- *a handful of coriander, chopped*
- *120 ml soy sauce*
- *1 tbsp cracked black pepper*
- *½ tsp crushed red pepper*

GARLIC FRIES

- *Bag of fries*
- *6 cloves of garlic, finely chopped*
- *½ tsp sea salt*
- *1/2 tsp cracked black pepper*
- *BBQ*
- *Ziplock bag*

METHOD (CARNE ASADA)

Cut the steak and place it in a large zip lock bag before adding the lime juice, garlic, soy sauce, coriander, bell pepper, and onions.

Agitate the bag to make sure the steak is completely covered with the ingredients and store in the fridge for an hour.

Discard the marinade and cook the steak over medium to high heat (about 4 minutes per side).

Remove from the grill and let relax for 10 minutes before slicing.

Method (garlic fries)

Cook the fries and season in the heat with salt, pepper, and garlic

Serve in a bowl and cover with the sliced meat.

Add your favorite toppings!

ABOUT THIS RECIPE

Lohikeitto is Finnish for "salmon soup" and is a common Dish in Scandinavian countries. This soup looks easy to prepare and tastes delicious.

121

LOHIKEITTO – FINNISH FISH SOUP

INGREDIENTS

- 2 tbsp mashed potatoes
- 2 tbsp whole milk powder
- ¼ tsp fish spice
- ¼ vegetable stock cubes
- 1 tablespoon of ghee
- 1 small shallot
- Salt and pepper
- 1 bay leaf
- 1 can (approx. 70 g) boneless pink salmon

what you will need

- Ziplock bag
- Pan
- spoons

METHOD

Put the mashed potatoes, fish seasoning, and powdered milk and crumble bouillon cubes in a ziplock bag and pack all other ingredients separately.

At Camp

Melt the ghee in the pan and add the chopped shallot. Cook until translucent and soft, then pour the mixture from the ziplock bag and mix with 120 ml of water.

Bring to the boil and stir occasionally. Season with salt and pepper and combinate it with bay leaf and salmon. Then simmer for 5 minutes before removing from the heat.

Throw away the bay leaf and enjoy!

ABOUT THIS RECIPE

This is an excellent and easy recipe that is ideal for hikers on the trail because it maintains the energy level. It is a nutritional power plant full of zinc, heart-healthy magnesium, several B vitamins, healthy Omega-3 fats, and antioxidants. It is perfectly portable and saves brilliantly!

122

MOREISH SEED TRAIL MIX

INGREDIENTS

- 200 g sunflower seeds
- 150 g pumpkin seeds
- 150 ml bottle of soy sauce

what you will need

- bowl
- Scree
- Sheet
- oven
- Airtight container

METHOD

This snack must be prepared at home in advance but will keep for days - ideal for long adventures.

Place the soy sauce in a bowl and stir in the sunflower seeds. Allow marinade for 10-15 minutes.

Drain the mixture through a sieve (you can reuse the remaining soy sauce) and spread the sunflower seeds evenly on a baking sheet.

Use a different baking stream for the pumpkin seeds.

Warm up the oven to 190C or Gas Mark 5 and roast the sunflower seeds for about 16 minutes. Roast the pumpkin seeds for 8 minutes.

Use a spatula to scrape the seeds off each tray airtightly Container. Close the lid and shake well.

The perfect partner when you are barbecuing on a beach, this salad is easy to prepare in advance. Put it in a big tub and let everyone help themselves!

123

NO COOK NOODLE SALAD

INGREDIENTS

PASTA SALAD

- *2 rice noodle nests*
- *6 spring onions or a little red onion*
- *1 red pepper*
- *1 yellow pepper*
- *1 carrot sliced sticks*
- *50 g chopped, fresh coriander*
- *100 g lightly roasted Cashews*

SESAME DRESSING

- *1 small clove of garlic, chopped*
- *1 inch of fresh ginger,*
- *2 tsp sesame oil*
- *2 tbsp lime juice*
- *2 tbsp soy sauce*
- *1 tsp refined sugar*
- *3 tablespoons of Thai chili sauce*

- *Large bowl*
- *Water heater*

METHOD

Add in 1 liter of boiling water the pasta and let rest for 8-10 minutes. Rinse and drain.

While the pasta has the red color cut during her wellness treatment

Onion/spring onions in thin slices.

Roast the cashew nuts carefully in a pan over medium heat for about 5 minutes. Often stir as they burn quickly. Let cool down.

Do the dressing in the medium bowl: combine the garlic, ginger, sesame oil, lime juice, soy, sugar, and sweet chili sauce. Stir until the sugar has dissolved.

Add the sliced onions to the dressing and let go 5 minutes.

Drain the soaked noodles and rinse them in cold water.

Mix all the ingredients in the medium-sized salad bowl with the dressing and stir gently and toss to combine.

Sprinkle with coriander and the roasted cashew nuts.

Store in a closed container in the fridge until needed or before three days have passed.

- *chopping board*
- *Knife*
- *Middle bowl*
- *Pan*
- *Lid container*

SURF HACK: Save on messy plates (plastic ones need packing and also washing up, and the wind seems to nick most of the paper ones),

Use large cabbage leaves as a container for the salad. They both look great and taste good too and can be locked with toothpicks (but be careful with children around). Tell the children that it is a new jungle rule! Tarzan would approve, and finally, the kids are on his lawn now.

If you have a sweet tooth, this recipe is ideal. The sweet pineapple is perfectly complemented by the crispy mint sugar to make a tempting; you won't be able to resist

124

SIZZLING PINEAPPLE WITH CRUNCHY MINT SUGAR

INGREDIENTS

- 1 ripe pineapple
- 1 tsp olive oil
- 8-10 g fresh mint leaves (chopped)
- 4 tsp castor sugar
- Greek yogurt for serving (optional)

what you will need

- Knife
- chopping board
- Pestle and mortar
- Cast iron frying pan
- baking gloves

METHOD

Take your beautiful fresh pineapple, cut off the top and bottom, and cut off the rest of the skin.

Quarter the fruit lengthways, cut the wooden core from each wedge, and then cut each quarter in half, leaving 8 long pieces.

Brush with the oil and place on a cast-iron skillet.

Once your campfire is nice and hot, brush it out gently hot embers and put the skillet on the embers. Allow the pineapple wedges to cook away for approx. 10 minutes and turn them over halfway.

Get a friend while keeping an eye on the pineapple to grind the mint leaves and sugar together in a pestle and mortar.

Do not add too much mint at first, as this makes grinding quite difficult.

Start with something and then add more leaves for a minty flavor.

Sprinkle as soon as the pineapple is browned on all sides, mint sugar on the slices, and add a pinch of Greek yogurt (if you fancy). Good Appetite!

SAUCES

Flame kitchen is an Alsatian tradition white top pizza and is basically a thin-crust Pizza that should be made with fresh cream, sliced onions, and smoked bacon.

125

WHITE TOP PIZZA SAUCE

INGREDIENTS

- *100 g full-fat fresh cream*
- *100 g natural yogurt*
- *Salt and pepper*
- *Freshly chopped coriander*

White lace sauce can be used with any kind of pizza, and you will see your family soon, and friends split into two camps: red top and white top. Please try it out; it will be worth it!

The best Steak Sauce Chimichurri originally comes from the Rio de la Plata, Argentina, and yet it is very green, very tasty, sweet, spicy, and fresh with a hint of heat.

126

CHIMICHURRI

INGREDIENTS

- 2 cups of fresh Italians parsley leaves
- 4 medium cloves of garlic - peeled and smashed
- ¼ cup of fresh oregano leaves
- ¼ cup of red wine vinegar
- ½ tsp red pepper flakes
- ½ tsp rock salt
- Freshly ground black pepper
- 1 cup of extra virgin olive oil

METHOD

Put your parsley, garlic, oregano, vinegar, red pepper flakes, salt, and pepper in a food processor.

Flash up until finely chopped for approx. a Minute. While still flashing, add the oil in a steady stream.

As with all sauces, it is best to at least cool for a couple of hours to allow the flavors to blend. Ideally, leave overnight.

ABOUT THIS RECIPE

This beautiful burger Sauce is a must prepared before Camping trip.

127

HOT PEANUT SAUCE

INGREDIENTS

- 1 medium onion and 2 small one's Chili peppers - finely chopped (including the seeds if you like it hot)
- 2 cloves of garlic
- 2 inch piece of grated ginger
- 2 tablespoons of good olive oil
- 1 tablespoon of toasted sesame oil
- 1 bowl of lime
- 2 cups of roasted peanuts
- 4 tbsp soy sauce
- ½ cup of water
- Season with salt and pepper

METHOD

Fry onions and chili peppers add to the oil until soft.

Season with garlic and ginger and cook for a few minutes.

Then stir in a blender until it is very smooth.

Put the remaining ingredients and whiz again until it's up to your like (we like our crispy).

128

CHICKEN KEBAB MALAI (CREAM)

INGREDIENTS

FOR THE KEBAB:

- 500 g boneless chicken - cut into small pieces
- ¼ cup of fresh double cream
- 2 tbsp of ginger bought in the store garlic paste
- 2 tablespoons bought in the store
- 1½ tsp salt
- 1 tsp vegetable oil
- Skewers

FOR CORIANDER AND MINT CHUTNEY:

- 2-3 tablespoons of yogurt
- A small handful of coriander & mint leaves
- Salt

METHOD

FOR THE KEBAB:

Mix ginger and garlic paste,

Rub in kebab masala, double cream, salt, and the marinade in the chicken.

At least let the marinated chicken rest a couple of hours in a cool place to make sure a cling film covers the chicken to ensure that no moisture is lost.

Once marinated, put the chicken pieces lightly on a skewer

Whisk some oil over it and then grill over a grill

(Depending on the size of the chicken, turn for 15 minutes every 5 minutes).

Once they're grilled a bit, they should be done.

FOR THE CORIANDER AND MINT CHUTNEY:

Chop the mint, and Coriander leaves are really fine, only as good as powder.

Add this to the yogurt and add some salt to the mixture.

Enjoy your kebabs with the yogurt dip.

129

SPICY CHICKPEA VEGETABLES

INGREDIENTS

- Rice of your choice
- 1 can of chickpeas
- 1 chopped carrot
- 1 onion
- 5 mushrooms
- 2-4 chili peppers to taste
- 1 spring onion
- 1 red pepper
- 2 cloves of garlic
- 2 tbsp tomato paste
- 1 tbsp turmeric powder
- 1 tbsp paprika
- Hot chili powder to taste

METHOD

Cook rice and set aside.

Open a can of chickpeas and put them in the pan.

Add a chopped carrot, an onion, 5 mushrooms, two Chili peppers, spring onions, a dash of red pepper and two cloves garlic in the pan with the chickpeas (you can actually add any vegetables you).

Add two tablespoons of tomato paste, one tablespoon of Turmeric powder, a tablespoon of paprika, and if you want to add more seasoning, add a couple of tablespoons of hot Chili powder or one or two additional chilies.

Pour a pint and a half of water into the pan and leave it there mix for a good 10-15 minutes or until bubbling

The chickpeas are soft and begin to shed their coatings.

Serve immediately.

130

ROASTED LAMB & VEGETABLES

INGREDIENTS

- Small leg of lamb.
- New potatoes
- Carrots - in large pieces
- Parsnips - cut into pieces
- Thyme
- Rosemary sprigs
- Vegetable oil
- Salt and pepper
- 2 cups of red wine
- 2 cups of cold water

METHOD

Marinate the lamb (you can use boned lamb) in a little oil, thyme, salt, and pepper. Illuminate the cobblestones according to the instructions, and when you're done, put the grill on the Cobb Barbecue to heat with the lid closed. Wipe the grill plate after 10 minutes with oil.

Mix the red wine and water together and pour a cup in the moat with the branches of rosemary.

Place the lamb in the grill plate center and let it steep 30 minutes. In the meantime, parboil the potatoes, parsnips, and Carrots. When you're done, throw in some oil and mixed herbs, salt, and pepper.

After 30 minutes, turn the lamb and put the potatoes, and place the carrots and parsnips around the lamb, check and fill the moat with more red wine and water. Turn the vegetables over

30 minutes. The lamb should take 1 hour 30 minutes to 1

Hour 45 minutes, depending on how you like it. Don't take the lid more than necessary; otherwise, you will lose heat.

If you use the roaster, you do not have to turn vegetables

Therefore, leave the lid open. Cooking times are reduced if you can resist the urge to take a look.

Remove the lamb and let it rest for 10 minutes whilst the vegetables stop cooking.